Generate Daily Income
from Financial Market -
Beginner's complete blueprint
of trading Binary options

Trading in financial markets for daily income
is much easier than you think.
Get started with this easy-to-follow blueprint.

Generate Daily Income from Financial Market -

Beginner's complete blueprint of trading Binary options

Sid Bhattacharjee

PARTRIDGE
A Penguin Random House Company

ISBN: Hardcover   978-1-4828-3864-0
            Softcover   978-1-4828-3863-3

Cover and back cover photo credit: Binu NG. of Binu Photography (www.binuphotography.com.au)

To order additional copies of this book, contact
Partridge India
000 800 10062 62
orders.india@partridgepublishing.com

www.partridgepublishing.com/india

CONTENTS

LIST OF FIGURES

This book is dedicated to those who inspired me to document my journey
through this fascinating world of financial markets,
and they are my beloved wife, Sumita, who is my courage, strength,
and inspiration; my boy, Shivayan; and my girl, Shivangi.

PREFACE

This book is pragmatic and not conceptual or theoretical. The book is intended for the readers to learn a new skill, a practical skill that, I think, could be of great value to any individual from any walk of life. The need to write this book has arisen from a number of factors described subsequently, but for now, let me tell you that I have had gone through a period of time in my life that inspired me to learn a subject that I never had any background on or had any resources to learn from or any mentor to coach me on. I had embarked on a journey all alone, but the journey has enriched my life in many aspects—some related, some unrelated. But I surely count those a great value addition to my life.

I have also been inspired by many of my family, friends, and colleagues who have been, or are, in a situation popularly called rat race, which they had slipped into either unknowingly or by force. They sometimes endeavoured to come out of this position but do not know how. I have been there too. This book is an effort to help the readers learn a skill that may open up a new avenue in front of them and alleviate their position in some way.

This book introduces a practical concept and a road map for any ordinary individual to learn how to earn a daily income from the financial market using a relatively new instrument called binary options, which is also called digital options or all-or-nothing options. While the book was written after being inspired by my wife, one of the many stay-home mums around the world, I see this being useful for anyone—be it a student, retiree, self-employed, or regular-employed person—aspiring to add a stream of regular income or replace their current income.

In my journey to learn about financial markets and trading various instruments, I have gone through peaks and troughs of a range of emotions. As a first-generation trader, it started to take a toll on my life as I was not attuned to handle those emotions. For example, when I started trading CFD across three major stock markets around the world (Australia, UK, and US), I found myself looking at the Bloomberg app on my iPhone all the time to check how the market is going and what effect it would have on my portfolio of positions. I used to wake up in the middle of the night and would be looking at the Bloomberg watch list I created on my iPhone to see the net open positions.

One day, while driving to work, I realized that in one of the short positions in a US stock CFD, I had lost my full investment and more as the company got a takeover offer from its competitor and share prices went up by over 10% overnight. By the way, in short positions, you could end up losing money if share prices go up, contrary to traditional belief that money can be made when share prices go up. I wanted to get better than this in terms of getting back my life and not having to keep an eye on the watch list 24 hours a day, 5 days a week. It is this motivation that I started to look for a simple methodology to continue with my passion for financial markets.

As a full-time employee with two young children, it is often hard to find time to write anything, let alone a book, but I have an exceptionally tolerant and understanding family, who motivated me to pen down my experiences on my journey. My family remains the nucleus of what I do, and needless to say, I am incredibly grateful to my wife (Sumita), my son (Shivayan), and daughter (Shivangi) for letting me do what I have so much passion for.

My main motivation for this book is my wife, Sumita, as she thinks that I should share my learning with others as there are millions of people like me who would have gone through the roller-coaster rides of their lives and not know what to do and that my book should give them some hope. I thought she was right as the book may save years for someone who would like to have a daily income from a source that all of us have access to but on which we do not know where to start. So along with some introductory concepts of the financial market, this book is intended to be a first step towards the fascinating world of financial markets.

Every possible care has been taken to lay down a detailed plan or road map to include all the tools you need, the advanced concepts available to improve your chances of success, and most importantly, the mental preparation to handle adverse situations. All these are followed by my personal record of trading history so you would know that I am not presenting a theoretical concept but a blueprint that has been put to the test.

Finally, I have put together a four-week action plan that has been designed to get the readers of this book underway with confidence. My sincerest urge is that the readers stick to the four-week action plan as much as possible so that definite results could be seen and measured.

Additionally, please also visit my website www.generatedailyincome.com for any additional resources, comments, and suggestions. I would also like to hear from you about your experience in trading and how you are getting on with the plan. So do drop me a mail via the website, and I will endeavour to reply individually. Please do allow some time for response.

ACKNOWLEDGEMENTS

duḥkheṣv anudvigna-manāḥ sukheṣu vigata-spṛhaḥ
vīta-rāga-bhaya-krodhaḥ sthita-dhīr munir ucyate

- Bhagavad Gita, Chapter 2, Verse 56

"One who is not disturbed in mind even amidst the miseries or elated when there is happiness, and who is free from attachment, fear and anger, is called a sage of steady mind."

I have grown up hearing this Lord Krishna's doctrine to Arjuna in the battlefield of Mahabharata from my late father Nilkantha Bhattacharjee, the lesson that remains deeply ingrained in my heart and soul even today. No amount of words is going to explain his contributions in my life. He is no more with us but surely his blessings have been with me all the way.

I also do not have enough words to describe the contribution of my mother late Supriti Bhattacharjee who had not only ensured that the family runs like a well oiled machine but also that myself and my two other siblings had received proper education in our formative years. She lived her life like a candle that burnt itself but gave light to others so that the family could flourish.

Many people and organisations have made direct and indirect contribution in writing of this book in form of support and encouragement. I am indebted to each one of them as without their support, it would have been impossible to be motivated to write the book. Thank you and I sincerely acknowledge your contribution.

ABOUT THE AUTHOR

Siddhartha Bhattacharjee, or Sid Bhattacharjee as he is called by his friends and colleagues, is a first-generation trader. He comes from a family of academicians and engineers. Sid's grandfather was a renowned Sanskrit scholar in the city of Dibrugarh of the state of Assam in India, originally migrating from East Bengal of the then undivided India. His father served at the Indian Railways for over 40 years. Many of his family members are spread around the world and are engaged in a variety of professions, including teaching in universities.

In his professional life, Sid has been a research scientist working with Government of Assam and Government of India in various research laboratories developing industrial automation, SCADA and telemetry projects. During that time, Sid has also been a part-time lecturer in several engineering institutes in India teaching industrial electronics. He had worked for global electronic giant Motorola as systems engineer designing cellular networks and later as a regional business head in their European cellular infrastructure division based on Kolkata, India. During his association with Motorola, Sid has also been teaching mobile data network architecture in the EMEA region. Sid is currently working with mobile carrier Vodafone in their Global Enterprises division. Sid has also delivered guest lecture at University of New South Wales (UNSW) on enterprise mobility.

Sid had started his private trading career in 2009, starting with CFD (contract for difference), a derivative product that entails a very high risk but also very high rewards. He also traded currency and futures in between. He enjoyed trading equity options in its simple form with Australian equities and also in a little more sophisticated form with US equities and indices. Currently, Sid trades only CFDs and binary options whenever he finds time. His interest includes statistical arbitrage trading and general algorithmic trading in equities and currencies.

Sid is an electrical engineer with a bachelor's degree from Gauhati University in India. He also had his MBA in finance from Macquarie Graduate School of Management, Sydney. Sid is currently based in Sydney, Australia, with his family, consisting of his wife and two children. Sid is a licensed amateur radio operator since his college days and also has an interest in sports, music, art, and culture.

DISCLAIMER

Trading in financial markets has large potential rewards, but also it has large potential risks. You must be aware of the risks and be willing to accept them in order to trade. Don't trade with money you can't afford to lose. This is neither a solicitation nor an offer to buy/sell any of the financial instruments mentioned in this book.

No representation is being made that any account will or is likely to achieve profits or losses similar to those shown. The past performance of any trading system or methodology is not necessarily indicative of future results.

The information provided in this book or website linked to this book is for educational purposes only and is not intended for providing financial advice. Any statements about profits or income, expressed or implied, do not represent a guarantee. You accept full responsibility for your actions, trades, profit, or loss and agree not to hold the author responsible in any and all ways.

The trading-platform examples shown in this book are from IG Markets, Stockpair, and Core Liquidity Markets (CLM Forex) for various reasons described in the chapters of this book. The author does not endorse any one of the brokerage firms offering these trading platforms. The author has been a customer of IG Markets for over five years. The author was granted access to Stockpair's and Core Liquidity Markets' trading platforms for the purpose of demonstration only. The author receives no commission from any of these

Sid Bhattacharjee

brokerage firms in any manner. The author pays normal commission to IG Markets for trading any other trading product, such as CFD or equity options. There are no commissions charged for trading digital or binary options by any of these three brokerages.

INTRODUCTION

Now that I have your attention, let me tell you something about the motivation behind the book. Why am I telling you this? I think you should know this not because this is a story you might like but because you might be able to relate to this story in some form or shape or just give you a reason to be motivated to take a step beyond your day-to-day routine.

I have known my wife, Sumita, for three years before we got married. She was in her high school years then, and I was a young engineer in my first job straight after graduation. Immediately after our marriage, she was diagnosed with kidney stones. After years of medication and treatment from some of the experts in the area, she got better. A couple of years later, our son was born. Usually, pregnant women develop high blood pressure before childbirth, but the blood pressure usually becomes normal after childbirth. In my wife's case, the latter didn't happen, and she went on medication for hypertension at a very young age. Her new health condition prevented her from going outside and taking any job or being involved in any sort of business. That's how we settled in our young married life in Kolkata with a newly born child.

Life took twists and turns over the years, and we found ourselves in our new home country with a brand-new job. Immediately after landing in the new job, the first turbulence hit. With mass redundancy across the company, many of the overseas recruits had to go back home. I had no clue as to what we would do if I lost the job and had to go back, uncertain in an alien country and with no family and friends to seek help from. History repeated again after a few years, but then, I had a few ideas in my mind on how to survive.

I started learning to trade in the financial market. I studied books, attended classroom lectures, listened to experts on TV, and developed a deep love towards this whole new aspect of business that I knew existed but didn't have any background on. As I learnt, I discussed all these with Sumita, who also developed a lot of interest on the subject. Our immediate thought was that if Sumita could learn to trade in the financial markets, she could do all these from the comfort of our home, something which both of us wanted. As for me, at least I now know that I could face challenges with a little bit more confidence and survive if I would ever be in a situation beyond my control.

To give you an idea of the range of markets and strategies that I have learnt and traded over the years, it included CFD (contract for difference), a highly profitable instrument with very high risks; equity options, a derivative of stock trading but with a limited-risk strategy; foreign exchange (forex); futures; and so on. Each of these took me a while to learn, but reading books and attending trainings, seminars, and lectures have enriched me like never before, and it gave me a better picture of the apparently complex financial market. At the same time, I also noticed that you need to have a simple orientation of mind to trade successfully and don't need to have a complex or convoluted strategy to take a position in the financial market and get a decent return.

With all these in my mind and inspired by the possibilities, I decided to document my experiences in a book so that new entrants to the financial market could benefit without having to go through all that I had gone through. This book is all about a no-nonsense approach to trading and making some money, I promise. I couldn't be any more straightforward than this. I had to write this book with my wife, Sumita, in mind as she has no prior exposure to any form of trading or anything to do with the financial markets. So the language used in this book is simple—no jargons or acronyms or any complicated terminology or systems.

The book contains no fluff or beating around the bush, so to speak; it is intended to provide a cut-to-the-chase road map for someone with no experience. Admittedly, some may take longer to learn than others, but you will get there with a bit of practice. The book includes an introduction to financial markets, with a brief for the various instruments that are traded in those markets.

Many of this information is available in the public domain, such as the Internet, books, journals, and TV. But I decided to include all these in the book for one simple reason: for a new entrant into the financial market who has no idea of what to look for and where to look to be provided with a succinct compilation of some basic information on financial markets through this book.

Out of all I learnt in the previous years, I found one particular type of trading that requires the least prior education or knowledge and suits those who are disciplined. I am making no promises of how much money you will make and in how much time, but I can assure you that the new skill that you are going to learn from this book will have a significant positive impact if you are disciplined.

Please do not treat trading as gambling, but if you do, please stop reading now. I have devoted a separate chapter on mental preparation for this— or, as a matter of fact, any type of trading—simply because trading has an extraordinarily high risks and high returns. Your mental strength and discipline are required to manage risks, minimize losses, and accumulate on the gains. There is no trading that exists in this planet that will not result in occasional losses. It's all about keeping the losses to a minimum and making gains more pronounced so that the net result is a profit, and this can be achieved by putting the odds in your favour, so to speak.

One more thing that I would like to emphasize here before I get into the crux of the subject is, as far as I am aware, there are no college or university educational courses available on this subject or any subject on trading in financial markets. Universities offering actuarial studies course teach plenty of theoretical concepts on mathematics, statistics and econometrics related to financial markets and deciphering the numbers in financial statements of publicly listed companies for investment decisions but nothing on hands-on trading in financial markets. Over the years, while I was learning and looking for information over the Internet and talking to people, I came across a variety of companies, businesses, organizations who deliver training on various styles of trading across a range of financial markets. The training courses offered by those organizations range from one-on-one mentoring to three-day to five-day face-to-face classroom delivery and online coaching. Some of them offer ongoing mentoring services with a monthly subscription as well. The prices range from $2,000 an hour to between $5,000 and $20,000 for a three-to-five-day course. I am not going to comment on the quality of training and the learning experience as I haven't attended any of those, but surely, I think that an upfront training cost of that magnitude would be significant for most starters, including myself.

So I decided to share my learning through this book so that the readers can invest the money in trading rather than committing a large sum for training alone. I agree that one-on-one coaching perhaps have better value than reading a book, but my intention is to ensure that new traders stepping out in the financial market for the first time will start with some solid foundation on which they can build their expertise at a fraction of the costs involved. If readers grasp the basic concepts enumerated in this book, then not only can they learn a new skill but can also step up to learn other related skills required to trade successfully in financial markets.

While writing this book, I wanted to make sure that the contents of this book are designed for someone with no previous background in financial markets. I have read several books, journals, reports, and so on; most of those delve into theories or complicated mathematical models or downright conceptual things that although may help beginners learn a few things but not to the extent that can help them acquire knowledge and skills to start trading in financial markets. I sincerely hope that, through the chapters of this book, readers are imparted practical knowledge and hands-on steps to get started.

So good luck, and thanks once again for purchasing this book and investing a small amount in learning a great new skill.

CHAPTER 1
What Is This All About?

I am going to be brutally simple and straightforward on this, and there is no greater truth than this. If you think that trading requires inside knowledge, that you need huge information, and that only those who have inside knowledge can only be successful, I would like you to completely dispel that from your mind. And I tell you, the sooner you stop thinking of that, the better prepared you will be for trading in the financial market, particularly the type of trading discussed in this book. I agree that certain types of trading will benefit from inside knowledge but not the type of trading discussed in this book. I am not going to go to all the details of the various other types of trading. This could be a subject for my future book, but for now, I would keep it simple and stupid (KISS), and that's what you should be focusing on.

Let's go straight into the subject and begin with an example. We almost always keep an eye on the currency conversion rate in one way or the other, either intentionally as we travel overseas or unintentionally through the newspaper or radio or TV. Let's take the example of the conversion rate of European Union's currency, euro (EUR), to the United States' dollar (USD), which is represented by EURUSD in financial markets.

You need to answer one simple question: is the value of euro going *up* or *down* against the US dollar in the next 5 or 10 or 20 minutes or an hour?

Here's another version of the question above: is EURUSD going to be *high* or *low* in the next 5, 10, 20, or 60 minutes? Or is the EURUSD price going to be *above* or *below* the current value in the next 5, 10, 20, or 60 minutes?

All the above are basically the same questions asked differently, but you got the idea. If you rightly guess the answer, you will have between 72% to 81% return on your investment, or you will get around $172 to $181 for every $100 you invest. If you are wrong, you will lose 100% of your investment or the full $100.

Does this thought excite you or scare you? Or you might think it is a statistical probability question and you could be right 50% of the time, just like the type of result you would expect when you toss a coin.

If you think it is a statistical probability question, then you are on track to be a good trader as you are most likely to get your decision right at least 50% of the time. But that's not good enough as you will soon find out that being right 50% will land you in a loss overall. So you need to be correct slightly more than 50% of the time to make break-even or obtain returns to cover for the losses. If your decisions are correct even a higher percentage of the time, then returns from your investment will cover for your losses, and you will be left with a net profit after covering for the losses.

This book aims to put the odds in your favour so that you are right well above 50% of the time. I am going to provide you only as much as you need to make your decisions correct more than 50% of the time so that you have a daily positive net profit from your decisions. Over time you can grow your trading account, and if you are disciplined, the account will grow faster.

To explain what I mean from above, I have painted a few scenarios for you so that you can appreciate what I am trying to get across to you.

Table 1 Possible returns with various percentage of winning trades

Total trades	Winners	Losers	Amount won	Amount lost	Net profit/loss
10	5	5	$400	$500	–$100
10	6	4	$480	$400	$80
10	7	3	$560	$300	$260
10	8	2	$640	$200	$440
10	9	1	$720	$100	$620
10	10	0	$800	$0	$800

The assumptions in the Table 1 are:

Investment in each trade: $100
Winning return per trade: 80%
Losing return per trade: –100%

You could potentially use $100 per trade or more or less (minimum and maximum investment per trade varies with brokers) and see for yourself what your earning potential could be for various percentages of winning trade.

This type of trading is called binary options. It is sometimes also called digital options or all-or-nothing options. Although the example here deals with currency as the underlying market, you could trade binary options with shares or share indices or commodities as underlying market, depending upon the range of markets your broker offers. Some details of these alternative instruments will follow in Chapter 2.

If the above makes sense to you, please hang in there. I will share all that you need to move from 50% to 60% or more in making correct decisions. To make it clean and simple, we are going to learn to put the odds in our favour so as to make the decision outcome better than tossing a coin.

I will talk you through the tools you will need and where to find those, how much you should invest to start with, when to trade, and what markets to trade in. I will also show you some of the results that you might expect, which are from my own daily statements from the broker.

We will also talk about the possible brokers to use in this trading method and the set-up you would need.

And finally, we will learn how to manage the money, how much money to trade, and how to manage losses.

We will put together everything that we have learnt into a trading system that works.

— **End of Chapter 1** —

CHAPTER 2

The Market:
Financial Markets of the World

You have seen the word *market* being used so many times in the previous chapter. What is that after all?

Market, in simple terms, means 'a place where people buy or sell some types of products'. Financial market is a place where people buy or sell financial products. What are financial products? This requires a bit of consideration, and I am going to explain the financial markets and financial products in the simplest possible terms so that you will have a fairly good understanding of it and you can make informed decisions about trading in those markets in the future if you want to. But note that the information provided are only for your general knowledge more than anything else as you will not need to know these for the simple trading system I am describing in this book.

Shares or Equity Market

Share or equity is a single unit of ownership of a public company. Shares of private companies are not available to ordinary individuals for selling or purchasing. Typically, apart from a small ownership by individuals, big investors buy and sell shares in a public company, which include hedge funds, superannuation funds, mutual funds, banks, etc. By buying shares in a company, you become a part-owner of the company, or a shareholder, however infinitesimally small that share ownership may be.

Shares of public companies are listed for trading in stock exchanges around the world. For example, most Australian companies' shares are listed in the Australian Stock Exchange (ASX), American companies' shares are listed either in the New York Stock Exchange (NYSE) or NASDAQ or AMEX, and British companies' shares are listed in the London Stock Exchange (LSE). There are some companies whose shares are listed in multiple stock exchanges. For example, BHP Billiton Ltd (BHP) shares are listed in the LSE and NYSE, and so are the shares of Rio Tinto Ltd (RIO) and those of a few others.

Shares are identified by symbols and these usually have three or four letters. As stated above, BHP Billiton Ltd's company shares are listed as BHP in the Australian Stock Exchange. It is also listed as BLT in the London Stock Exchange. Wesfarmer Ltd's (owner of Coles supermarket in Australia) company shares are listed in the Australian Stock Exchange as WES. Popular Internet book retailer Amazon is listed in the New York Stock Exchange as AMZN. Another popular company, eBay (difficult to believe that it has not touched our lives in one way or the other), is also listed in the American Stock Exchange and NASDAQ as EBAY and the list goes on.

For an individual investor to buy and sell shares, you will need to engage a broker to do the transaction on your behalf. Some of the well-known brokers are Commonwealth Securities, Scottrade, E*TRADE, and Charles Schwab. You will need to open an account with one of the brokers to start trading. Please note that some brokers allow trading only in domestic shares and not overseas shares, whereas some international brokers allow trading shares in stock exchanges all around the world.

Shares could be purchased in any denomination (such as 100 shares, 200 shares, and 500 shares) or odd lots (such as 440 shares or 225 shares). The reason one might have a multiple of 100 shares is because, in another market (to be described later in this section), 100 shares form one contract. Investors might have odd lots because sometimes companies issue additional shares to existing shareholders or the investors might have been assigned an odd number of shares as part of the IPO (initial public offering), a process by which a company goes public by listing their shares for the first time in a stock exchange.

When you are a shareholder, you may be entitled to dividends. Dividends are residual profits earned by a company from the business it is engaged in and are usually paid to shareholders on a per-share basis. Some companies may not pay dividends either because of poor performance of the company or because they needed the money to invest for a project which may in turn bring a larger profit in the following years. In Australia, dividends are paid to shareholders after company taxes are deducted and often mentioned as fully franked. This means you as a shareholder do not need to pay tax once again for your personal income. This avoids double taxation on the same income—once, when the company earns a profit and, another time, when a dividend is earned by an investor when the company distributes its profits in the form of dividends.

Blue-chip shares: You might often come across the term 'blue-chip shares'. Suffice to say that these shares are generally that of top companies which are highly valued in terms of market capitalization (number of shares issued times the market price of each share). These companies are also part of the stock index of the share exchange. Stock index is a single number that's used to represent the general direction of the stock market and is calculated using a variety of methods depending upon the specific stock exchange and using the share prices of usually blue-chip companies. In Australia, the share index is called All Ordinaries. Other indices are S & P 500, Dow, etc. There are indices used to indicate the general direction of the share market for specific types of companies, such as mining, pharmaceuticals, and engineering. We are not going through each of them, but suffice to say that blue-chip shares are used for calculating all these indices.

In the Australian market, examples of blue-chip shares are BHP, RIO, WOW, WES, CBA, and ANZ. In NYSE, examples of blue-chip shares are APPL(Apple), EXON (Exon mobil), PFI (Pfizer), and HPQ (Hewlett-Packard).

Share buy-back: As part of the company's financial restructure, sometimes companies buy back their own shares from shareholders at market price or at premium. That's one way of giving the money back to the shareholders. This is usually optional, and shareholders may opt in or opt out, but I don't see any reason why a shareholder wouldn't sell their shares at a premium when the same shares may be available at a discounted price later, which usually happens after a big share buy-back by companies.

Merger and acquisition: A whole company is sometimes up for sale, or a company makes an offer to buy another company. Usually, such offers to buy involve paying a significant premium depending upon the market standing of the company. If you are holding a share of a company that has received an offer to be bought by another company, then you will usually be given the option to exchange your shares for cash or to exchange your shares for the shares of the buying company of similar value. Often such mergers and acquisitions give a significant opportunity to make a quick big profit because of the premium paid by the buying company to the target company's shareholders.

CFD or Contract for Difference

CFDs are a special kind of shares which are not traded in stock exchanges but are offered for trade by CFD providers as an over-the-counter product. CFD providers are also a kind of regular brokers who may provide a trader various other instruments apart from CFDs for trading. CFD is a leveraged product, meaning that for every buy or sell transaction of a CFD product, you will need to put up only a small amount of margin money and not the full cost of the shares. For example, if you were to buy 100 CFDs of BHP—which is currently trading in the Australian Stock Exchange at, say, $40 per share—you will be required to pay only $200 as margin money and not $4,000 ($40 times 100), assuming the required margin is 5%.

A CFD provider provides you the fund needed to pay for buying those BHP shares; in exchange, they will collect interest from you, usually slightly higher than the local central bank's interest rate. Let's say after buying those 100 BHP CFDs, the BHP shares creep up higher in the next few days, and the new share price is $42 per share. In that case, you would have made a profit of $200 ($2 increase per share for 100 shares) from an investment of $200. That's 100% return on investment! Sounds good, doesn't it? Let's say BHP shares fall to $37 in the next few days after you bought the CFDs. In that case, you would have lost $300 ($3 loss per share for 100 shares). That's more than 100% of your investment. This is an example to show that with CFDs, you could lose more than your investment.

As you see from the examples above, CFDs are a very high-risk instrument but capable of providing very high returns. There are sound trading strategies that traders use to mitigate those downside risks but still keep the upside intact. New traders are not advised to trade CFDs without having a full understanding of the risks and rewards of trading this leveraged instrument and without having a good plan to manage their investments.

Because of the nature of the risks involved, CFDs are not available to trade in some countries—notably, the US. CFDs are, however, allowed for trading in Australia and in some parts of Europe. Depending upon the CFD provider, CFDs could be traded on a range of underlying shares traded across most major stock exchanges around the world. Even though CFD trading is not allowed in the US, a trader in Australia or Europe could use shares traded in US stock exchanges as underlying assets for CFD trading. For example, a trader in Australia could trade CFDs on eBay, which is traded in NYSE.

Various CFD providers offer to trade CFDs with a range of underlying shares with different levels of margins. Some blue-chip shares will need a much lower margin, such as 5%, whereas some other shares might need a margin as high as 40%. The margins required by the CFD providers usually depend upon the liquidity (meaning, the volume of shares traded per day) of the underlying shares, the industry to which the company belongs, market capitalization (share prices times the number of shares sold by the company), and such factors. BHP, RIO, etc., being blue-chip shares, requires much smaller margins than other shares.

In Australia, there are several CFD providers—such as IG Markets, CMC Markets, and City Index—apart from large banks, such as CommSec.

Share Indices

All stock exchanges use some form of index to indicate the sentiment in the market. The index has a name and is in the form of a number. The number is actually derived from the share prices of blue-chip shares and a few other parameters specific to the stock exchange. For example, the index of the Australian Stock Exchange (ASX) is called All Ordinaries or XAO in the stock exchange code. At the writing of this book, All Ordinaries had a value of about 5,200. As various shares in the Australian stock market move, the All Ordinaries Index would assume different values.

There are also indices based on specific categories of shares belonging to various sectors. For example, an index made up of shares from the material sector in Australian stock exchange is called material index or XMJ in stock exchange code. The index of shares from medium-sized companies in Australia is called S & P/ASX MidCap 50 or, in stock exchange code, XMD. Similarly, the share index of the American market is called DJIA, or Dow Jones Industrial Average. As a matter of fact, there are a few other indices in America; one of the most popular ones is S & P 500. The stock index of London Stock Exchange (LSE) is called FTSE and so on and so forth. Please note that these indices are purely for the purpose of indicating the general direction of the shares being traded at those exchanges.

There is another class of indices which is tradable, meaning you can buy and sell those indices. But the question is, what do you get when you buy or sell those indices? These tradable indices mostly mimic the main index of the stock exchange. For example, S & P/ASX 200 is a tradable index in the Australian Stock Exchange. The index is made up of the top 200 shares traded in Australia. So when you buy the index, you are buying a basket of those 200 shares represented as a certain percentage of the total amount you are investing. Since it is impractical for the exchange to deliver 200 shares to a buyer, the indices are cash-settled. This means that when you buy and sell the index, you will make a profit or loss depending upon whether or not the index has moved up or down.

One of the biggest advantages of trading indices is that a trader is not exposed to the risks associated with one individual share price movement. For example, if one of the 200 shares plummets because of some major issues, it is unlikely to affect the general movement of the index price, or the effect will be much less pronounced had you been holding just one position with that share. Of course, the index price movement will be greater if all shares making up the index follow the price movement in the same direction.

Traders use a variety of strategies to trade indices. Some use such indices to hedge their position while some trade indices as they are and make money from small movements of the index price.

Commodities

Commodities are the raw materials humans use to create a liveable world. Commodities are most often used as inputs in the production of other goods or services. Humans use energy to sustain themselves, metals to build weapons and tools, and agricultural products to feed themselves. Such are the essential building blocks of humankind.

Commodities are usually classified in the forms of energies, metals, grains, livestock, etc. and are traded worldwide as part of global trade. Energy commodity includes various types of crude oils. Metals include gold, silver, palladium, and platinum. Grains include soybeans and oats. Livestock includes cattle, and soft commodities include cocoa, coffee, sugar, and orange juice.

Commodities are usually traded in a separate type of exchange, and there are only a few in the world, unlike stock exchanges. A commodities exchange is an exchange where various commodities and derivatives of products are traded. Most commodity markets across the world trade in agricultural products and other raw materials (like wheat, barley, sugar, maize, cotton, cocoa, coffee, milk products, pork bellies, oil, and metals) and contracts based on them.

Commodities exchanges usually trade futures contracts, the details of which are in the following section. A farmer growing corn can sell a futures contract to deliver his corn of a certain volume in a certain month in the future. A breakfast cereal producer buys the contract now and guarantees the price will not go up when it is delivered. This protects the farmer from price drops and the buyer from price rises.

One of the major commodities exchanges in the world is the CME Group in United States, created by merger between CME (Chicago Mercantile Exchange) and CBOT (Chicago Board of Trade), which trades grains, ethanol, metals, and others. Similarly, Singapore Mercantile Exchange or SMX Singapore trades precious metals, base metals, agricultural products, energy, etc.

Many people have become very rich by trading in the commodity markets. It is one of the few investment areas where an individual with limited capital can make extraordinary profits in a relatively short period of time. Nevertheless, because most people lose money, commodity trading has a bad reputation as being too risky for the average individual. The truth is that commodity trading is only as risky as you want to make it.

Futures

Futures in financial markets refer to futures contracts. A futures contract is a standardized contract between two parties to buy or sell a specified asset, such as a commodity, of standardized quantity and quality for a price agreed upon today with delivery and payment occurring at a specified future date, which is also called the delivery date.

The contracts are negotiated at a futures exchange, which acts as an intermediary between the two parties—as opposed to stock exchange where stocks are traded. The party agreeing to buy the underlying asset in the futures contract is called the *buyer* of the contract, and the party agreeing to sell the asset in the future is called the *seller* of the contract.

In trading terminology, the buyer is termed as being in a 'long' position, whereas the seller is termed as being in a 'short' position. These terms apply for trading in general as well. So when you buy some shares in anticipation of making a profit when the share prices go up, you are in a long position. The terminology reflects the expectations of the parties to make a profit such that the buyer hopes or expects that the underlying asset price is going to increase while the seller hopes or expects that it will decrease in the near future.

In many cases, the underlying asset to a futures contract is not the traditional commodities at all. For example, in financial futures, the underlying item can be any financial instrument, such as currency, bonds, and stocks. Futures contracts can also be based on intangible assets or referenced items, such as stock indices and interest rates.

While the futures contract specifies a trade taking place in the future, the purpose of the futures exchange institution is to act as intermediary and minimize the risk of default by either party. Thus, the futures exchange requires both parties to put up an initial amount of money as security, which is also called margin money. Additionally, since the futures price will generally change daily with the change of demand and supply of the underlying commodity, there will be a difference in the previously agreed price and the daily futures price; that difference in price is settled daily.

The net difference in margin caused by this variation in the daily price is called variation margin. The commodities exchange will draw money out of one party's margin account and put it into the other party's margin account so that each party has the appropriate daily loss or profit. If the margin account goes below a certain value, then a margin call is made to ask the account owner to replenish the margin account. This process is known as marking to market. Thus, on the delivery date, the amount exchanged is not the specified price on the contract but the spot value. This is because any gain or loss has already been previously settled by marking to market.

It is possible to exit the commitment prior to the settlement date of the futures contract; the holder of a futures position can close out its contract obligations by taking the opposite position on another futures contract on the same asset and settlement date. The difference in futures prices is then a profit or loss.

Futures are traded with a variety of underlying products ranging from stocks and commodities to currencies and bonds.

Bonds

Most investors are familiar with the one primary type of investment; that is stocks. Stocks are relatively easy to understand because we hear about the stock market on a daily basis. The news constantly reminds us about whether the stock market is going up, down, and what companies are doing the best and worst. What about bonds? We hear very little about bond markets or how these financial instruments actually work.

When you buy a share of stock, you buy a small piece of ownership of a corporation. The value of that stock fluctuates based on what investors or the market as a whole feel the company is worth. A bond is quite different. When you buy a bond, you're not buying ownership of a company, but instead, you're lending that company money. In return for your loan, the company pays you interest. Think of it as a bank loaning you money, only the roles are reversed. When you borrow money from the bank, the bank gives you a lump sum of money that you must repay over time with interest. That's exactly how a bond works, but this time you're the 'bank' lending money to a company, which then repays you over time and with interest.

While the above example describes a corporate bond, there are actually many different types of bond issuers. Not only can corporations issue bonds but so can the state, local, and federal governments.

Bonds are a little different from many other investments. With stocks, you're looking for capital appreciation. This means you want the price of your stock to go up. When you buy a bond, you're not as concerned with the increase or decrease of the bond price, but primarily looking to generate regular income in the form of interest.

That's not to say bond prices don't fluctuate—because they can—but they typically remain much more stable than the share price of a stock. Because of this relative stability in price and regular interest payments, bonds are considered safer investments than stocks.

Bonds are generally used by investors to offset some of the risk in their portfolio. Stocks can fluctuate from one day to the next by a significant margin, but bonds tend to remain fairly stable and, of course, pay out interest. So by adding bonds to your portfolio, you can mitigate some of the risks you're taking in stocks by having some stable income from bonds.

In real life, bonds are issued with coupons. Let's explain that with an example. If you were to invest $10,000 on a particular company's bond, then the company will issue you a certificate of $10,000, which is the amount of money that you are lending to the company, and a number of coupons. Each coupon represents an interest amount on the original investment of $10,000 at an agreed interest rate that you can redeem for cash every year or at an agreed interval till the time bond matures. So there is a cash flow for you every year, and the original investment is returned to you after maturity.

There is plenty of education available at colleges and universities on how to create a portfolio of investments using equities and bonds which has a certain risk profile and return. These are usually taught in business courses. I had one while I was doing my MBA. It was very interesting and has many practical uses. Many investment banks use these for designing an investment portfolio for people like you and me, where we can put our superannuation money or mutual fund.

Warrants

Warrants are securities that give the holder the right, but not the obligation, to buy a certain number of securities (usually the issuer's common stock) at a certain price before a certain time. Warrants are not the same as call options or stock purchase rights.

Public companies often offer warrants for direct sale or give them to employees as an incentive, but the vast majority of warrants are attached to newly issued bonds or preferred stock.

For example, if Company XYZ issues bonds with warrants attached, each bondholder might get a $1,000 face value bond and the right to purchase 100 shares of Company XYZ's stock at $20 per share at any time in the next five years. Warrants usually permit the holder to purchase common stock from the issuer, but sometimes they allow the purchaser to buy the stock or bonds of another entity, usually a subsidiary company or even a third party.

The price at which a warrant holder can purchase the underlying securities is called the exercise price or strike price. The exercise price is usually higher than the market price of the stock at the time of the warrant's issuance.

If the price of the stock is above the exercise price of the warrant, the warrant must have what is known as a minimum value. For example, consider the warrants to purchase 100 shares of Company XYZ for $20 per share anytime in the next five years. If Company XYZ's shares rose to $40 during that time, the warrant holder could purchase the shares for $20 each and immediately sell them for $40 on the open market, pocketing a profit of $2,000 (($40 – $20) × 100 shares). Thus, the minimum value of each warrant is $20.

It is important to note, however, that if the warrants still had a long time before they expired, investors might speculate that the price of Company XYZ's stock could go even higher than $100 per share. This speculation, accompanied by the extra time for the stock to rise further, is why a warrant with a minimum value of $20 could easily trade above $20. But as the warrant gets closer to expiring (and the chances of the stock price rising in time to further increase profits get smaller), that premium would shrink until it equalled the minimum value of the warrant (which could be $0 if the stock price falls below $20).

Companies often issue bonds and preferred stock with warrants attached as a way to enhance the demand and marketability of their stock offering. This is a smart way to lower the cost of raising capital for the issuer.

Forex

The forex market is one in which participants are able to buy, sell, exchange, and speculate on currencies or foreign exchanges. It is popularly called forex. Foreign exchange markets are made up of banks, commercial companies, central banks, investment management firms, hedge funds, and retail forex brokers and investors. The forex market is considered to be the largest financial market in the world with several trillion dollars worth of money changing hands every day.

The main trading centres for forex trading are New York and London; however, Tokyo, Hong Kong, and Singapore are also major centres as well. Major banks throughout the world participate in trading currencies. The forex market is open 24 hours a day and 5 days a week. Currency trading starts with an Asian session on Monday. As the Asian trading session ends, the European session begins. There is an overlap of the European session and the North American session for a few hours, following which the North American session continues till almost to the beginning of the Asian session on Tuesday. This goes on till the Friday close of the North American session.

Because the currency markets are large and liquid, they are believed to be the most efficient financial markets. It is important to note that the foreign exchange market is not a single exchange but is made up of a global network of financial institutions where computers connect various participants from all parts of the world.

Currencies are traded against one another in pairs. Each currency pair thus constitutes an individual trading product and is traditionally noted as

XXXYYY, where XXX and YYY are the international three-letter code of the currencies involved. The first currency is the base currency, which is quoted relative to the second currency or the quote currency. For instance, the quotation EURUSD 1.5465 is the price of the euro expressed in US dollars, meaning €1 = $1.5465.

Forex is traded in both spot market as well as in the futures market. Spot market is the one where a currency is quoted against another as of that instant.

On the spot market, the most traded currency pair is EURUSD, with almost a quarter of all forex transactions around the world. This is closely followed by USDJPY, which makes up over 18% of all forex transactions. And the third place is occupied by GBPUSD. Because of the sheer size of their economy, the US currency is involved in the bulk of the forex transactions, followed by the euro, the yen, and the sterling.

Fluctuations in currency exchange rates are usually caused by a variety of factors, such as actual monetary flows, expectations of changes in monetary flows caused by changes in gross domestic product (GDP) growth, inflation, interest rates, budget and trade deficits or surpluses, large cross-border M & A deals, and other such macroeconomic conditions.

Individual retail speculative traders constitute a growing segment of this market (both in size and importance) with the advent of retail foreign exchange platforms. Currently, they participate indirectly through brokers or banks. Retail traders trade forex in many different ways, the most popular being the simple buy or sell. A retail trader may buy one currency in anticipation of the currency to appreciate in time. If it goes up, they sell the currency and pocket the difference. This is called long trade.

Traders can also do a short trade on a currency, thus enter into a trade by selling a currency first by borrowing the currency from the broker. This is in anticipation of the currency to fall in value in future. If the currency value falls as expected by the trader, the trader buys the currency back at a lower value, thus pocketing the difference between the price at which he had sold first and the price at which he bought back later. Both long and short trades are managed by the broker, so as a trader, it is a simple transaction—either you are long or short.

In both transaction types mentioned above, the trader pays commission to the broker in the form of spread, which is the difference between the buy price and sell price or the ask price and bid price measured in pips. A pip is the smallest movement of price of a currency, which is usually the fourth digit after the decimal place of a quote. For example, if EURUSD is quoted as 1.5465 for bid and 1.5467 for ask, then the spread is 2 pips.

Forex is traded in lots: standard lot, mini lot, or micro lot. A standard lot is 100,000 of the base currency. For example, one standard lot of EURUSD would be worth the $100,000 equivalent in US dollars. A mini lot is one-tenth of a standard lot or 10,000 of the base currency. Similarly, a micro lot is one-hundredth of a standard lot or 1,000 of the base currency.

Brokers offer to trade forex in margin of various leverages, such as 1:100, 1:200, and 1:400. This means you will need to put up only a small fraction of the cost of one standard lot or one mini lot or one micro lot depending upon what size of trade your account was set up to trade and the leverage of your account. As an example, let's say you took a long position by buying one standard lot of the currency EURUSD at the current bid price of 1.5467 in anticipation of the price going up in the next few days. If your account leverage is 1:400, you will need to put up margin money of 1.5467 times 100,000 divided by 400 or US $386.68. If your account currency is anything other than US dollars, then the margin money will be calculated using the appropriate conversion rate from US dollars to that currency. But you get an idea that you need to come up with a small amount of money as margin to control a much larger amount of money.

Now let's say, in the next few days, EUR appreciates, and the ask price hits 1.5497. That is an increase of 30 pips. With one standard lot, each pip is worth US $10. So with a 30-pip appreciation, your profit on the trade is US $300 or a 77.6% return on investment. Surely, that is a significant return by any standard, and such returns are very common in forex trading and are achieved in a short span of time.

On the other hand, let's say the EUR depreciates, and the new EURUSD ask price is trading somewhere near 1.5427. This is a 40-pip drop in value or a loss of $400 (40 times $10). So on a margin of $386.68, you are facing a possible loss of $400. That's more than 100% of your margin! Of course, you wouldn't realize the loss until you close the trade. You may decide to hold on to the trade in anticipation of EURUSD going up soon. If the currency really starts moving up after the recent drop, then you will make a profit in the trade. But if the currency continues to go south, then you are exposed to a much bigger loss.

That's the reason traders often use a take-profit target (also called TP) and place a stop-loss position (also called SL) while placing a trade. Such orders give brokers the instruction to close the trade if the TP target is reached. Similarly, the brokers are also instructed to close off your trade if the trade goes against you and if the SL target is reached. Placing a take-profit target and stop-loss target is based on the strategy a trader uses, but the general practice is that the TP target is placed at 50% more than the SL target. As an example, if your SL is placed 20 pips below your entry point, then the TP is placed at least at 30 pips above the position at which the trade was opened, assuming you are in a long position (buying a currency pair). In this way, if you only have 50% successful trade, you will end up making money as your profits are going to be larger than the losses.

Because of the leverage, forex trading offers an extraordinary potential to make a profit in a short time and an equally very real opportunity for traders to lose money very fast as you just saw in the example. A trader will need to have a sound trading strategy coupled with a solid money management technique to be profitable in the long run. Most new entrants into forex trading are lured by very high returns and enter market with no proper plan on trade as well as on how to manage money. As a result of that, after they are hit by a string of losses, they quit the market and, most of the times, never come back again. Often, money management is more critical than the strategy as even with less than 50% successful trades but with the win size bigger than loss size, a trader can make very decent money.

Forex for Trading Binary Options

For the purpose of the trading method described in this book, we will focus on the forex market. Why? There are three main reasons—although you can use any other financial market for the purpose depending upon what markets are offered by your broker to trade binary options.

Here are the answers as to why I recommend you use forex as the instrument:

1. Although I have a preference for trading during certain times of the day, still it give you enough flexibility to choose your own suitable time without compromising your personal life and other priorities.

2. Because of the sheer volume of money trading in that market, there is significant volatility that is useful for the trading style described in this book. Higher volatility means that the prices move fast enough in a given time frame, such as one minute or five minutes, and you can make a decision on its possible movement in a particular direction based on its movement in previous time frames.

3. Forex is also very popular because of the size of the market and volume traded each day. It is offered by almost all brokers for trading binary options. As mentioned before, this is the single most popular financial market, where the number of its participants far exceeds the number of participants in equity market.

Just for the purpose of information, you might like to note that the commodities market also trade 24 hours a day, but the volume of trade is usually low or much lower compared to forex, and hence the volatility is not quite acceptable. On a longer time frame, it may be possible to trade in the commodities market the way we are going to learn to trade, but I do not recommend trading commodities for our kind of trading simply because of our choice of a lower time frame.

What is a time frame? *Time frame*, in relation to trading, just means 'a slice of time aligned with the reference clock or standard clock'. The slice of time could be from one minute to one week or even one month depending upon the trading style. For the trading method described here, we would be talking about five-minute to one-hour time frames and not daily or weekly as used by many stock or equity options traders.

The reference clock is one that is considered as the standard clock from which all other clocks are derived, such as the one from the NIST (National

Institute of Standards and Technology) available at www.time.gov. There are many other sources of reference clocks, such as the US Naval Observatory time available at http://tycho.usno.navy.mil/what.html or the Windows time service available at time.windows.com. Charts from all brokers will be aligned with one of these standard clocks so that each candle in any given time frame starts exactly in the same instant. They may, however, be shifted in time depending upon whether the broker follows the local time or UTC or any other time.

— **End of Chapter 2** —

CHAPTER 3

Digital Options or Binary Options

Binary options are a relatively new derivative product that has been introduced for trading by retail investors. These products are not traded in any stock or commodities exchanges but on the brokers' own servers with the data feed from the stock exchange for stock-based binary options or the commodities exchanges for commodities-based binary options or from major banks for forex-based binary options.

Binary means 'two states', like the binary numbers 0 and 1 used by computers. A binary option is a type of option where the return on investment is either some fixed amount of some asset or nothing at all, based on one of the two outcomes of an event. The two main types of binary options are the cash-or-nothing binary option and the asset-or-nothing binary option. The cash-or-nothing binary option pays some fixed amount of cash if the option expires in the money (or ITM, a term used to define that the price of the asset moved in the direction in which it was anticipated within a predetermined time after the investment was made) while the asset-or-nothing pays the value of the underlying security. Thus, the options are binary in nature because there are only two possible outcomes, the other outcome being out of money (or OTM, a term used to define that the asset price did not move in the anticipated direction on expiry of the predetermined time after the investment was made).

They are also called all-or-nothing options, digital options, or fixed-return options. Binary options are usually European-style options, meaning the options expire at a fixed time in the future and those options cannot be bought back or closed before expiry. The other exercise style in options is American, meaning, although the options expire at a fixed time in the future but those can be bought back or closed before expiry.

When trading binary options, the potential return it offers is certain and known before the trade is placed. Binary options can be bought on virtually any asset class and can be bought in both directions of trade either by buying a call/up option or a put/down option. If you recollect the introductory discussion in Chapter 1 on the concept of the trading to be discussed in this book, buying a *call* option is equivalent to placing a trade in anticipation of the price of the asset going *up*. Similarly, buying a *put* option is equivalent to placing a trade in anticipation of the price of the asset going down in the relevant time frame. This means that an investor can go long or short on any financial product simply by buying a binary option. Binary options are offered against a fixed expiry time, which may be 60 seconds, 5 minutes, 15 minutes, 30 minutes, an hour ahead, or to the close of the trading day.

Binary-options contracts were generally available over the counter for a long time, i.e. traded directly between the seller and the buyer. Because of these binary options contracts not being part of the mainstream trading in financial markets, the market for these options were not liquid, meaning there were not many buyers and sellers in the market. More frequently, these binary-options contracts were part of some other type of transaction in complex arrangements between a buyer and seller.

Binary options started becoming a popular instrument in financial markets sometime around 2008 when many brokers started offering a simplified version of the binary-options contract mentioned above. Most brokers offer a simple predetermined return on investment if the chosen asset goes *up* or *down* in a given time frame and if you had made the correct decision on the asset's movement. Some brokers offer the same or a different predetermined return on investment if the asset price only touched a predetermined price. Some brokers even offer some form of pair trading in which the trader receives a predetermined return if one asset performs better than the other over a given time frame. Most brokers of binary options offer no option to liquidate or close the trade before expiry while some do.

For the trading system we are going to learn in this book, we will use the simple form of binary options in which a predetermined return on investment is received from the broker if the asset price goes *above* or *below* the price at which the option was bought. This is not to say that the other types of binary options can't be traded with the method discussed in the book, but it is up to the readers to trade depending upon whether or not their broker offers those additional features or not.

With the mushrooming of brokers of binary options, various individuals and organizations came forward to lure retail traders to start trading with those brokers. As a result, there is no dearth in advertising and marketing materials out there in the Internet or otherwise. A simple search in the Internet will reveal what I mean. Many of the claims made by those individuals or organizations are downright misleading, and it is easy to fall prey to the lure of the tall claims made. Those tall claims are based on unachievable numbers of successful trades and traders requiring to take extraordinarily high risk, which is by no means considered reasonable by any standard. With the advent of the Internet, it is now possible to reach almost anyone and everyone through unsolicited mails and social media. So you may be surprised by how many mails or messages you might receive soliciting for your trade with those brokers.

With the increased popularity of binary options, the United States Securities and Exchange Commission (SEC) and Commodity Futures Trading Commission (CFTC) have issued a joint warning to investors regarding binary options. The main purpose of the warning is to keep the new entrants into binary-options trading informed of the possible risks involved and that claims made by the brokers or their representatives are often not representative of the possible returns available from trading binary options.

In this book, I will describe how to trade binary options because of its simplicity and readily available tools that anyone can use to make a decent daily income. Also, there are a relatively large number of brokers who now offer traders to trade binary options on a variety of platforms. In the following chapters, I will describe all those tools with examples from three brokers' platforms from which you can choose to trade with so that you are fully covered.

— **End of Chapter 3** —

CHAPTER 4
Market Analysis:
Fundamental or Technical?

Whenever you choose to trade in a financial market, you will need to have some understanding of how individual assets in that financial market are valued or what the sentiment in the market is to help you make a decision to buy or sell the asset. Your assessment of whether the asset is currently priced at high or low gives you an indication of whether the value in the future might go up or down.

For example, you assessed that the BHP shares are undervalued and that the sentiment is *bullish*, a term used to describe that the asset is going to appreciate in value. In that case, you would buy the share and look to sell the shares if the share price goes in your favour or goes up. On the contrary, if the share prices go against you, then you tend to lose money, but you wouldn't realize the loss till you sell the shares. Sometimes, it is possible that share prices take an adverse direction initially because of a variety of reasons but goes in your favour a little later. But how would you know whether you would need to hold on to the share a little longer to get a profit or you should sell the shares and take a loss?

An analysis of some form would perhaps reveal the picture and give traders some idea of where the share price is headed. The above is an example of the equity market, but the same applies for the equity derivative market as well, such as options, warrants, and equity index futures. And so are the other financial markets, such as forex and commodities market, if you are trading any of these assets.

In the forex market, for example, you may be keen to know how EURUSD is valued so that you could decide to buy EUR in anticipation of either the euro becoming stronger or the US dollar being weaker so that you could make money by selling euros at a later date. Similarly, if you are trading in the commodities market, you will want to know if the particular commodity you are trading is going to be influenced by some of the recent economic events and the corresponding sentiment in the financial market.

These are some of the examples of why you should be keen to know what is happening in your chosen financial market so that you can pick the right asset to trade and when to trade or even how to trade in terms of the strategy to employ. Traders use fundamental analysis or technical analysis or both to make those assessments. If you do not want to spend time on any of these analyses, then there are professional reports available from a variety of organizations that will provide you the fundamental, technical, or combined analyses for a fee. The Australian Stock Report (ASR), Morningstar, and Eureka Report are some of the examples of reports available in Australia apart from the reports from big players in financial markets, such as Bloomberg, Thomson Reuters, and similar organizations.

Fundamental Analysis

The fundamental approach is based on an in-depth and all-around study of the underlying forces of the economy, which is conducted to provide data that can be used to forecast future prices and market developments. Fundamental analysis can be composed of many different aspects: the analysis on the economy as a whole, the analysis on an industry, or the analysis on an individual company. A combination of the data is used to establish the true current value of the stocks, to determine whether they are overvalued or undervalued, and to predict the future value of the stocks based on this information.

Fundamental analysis is considered to be the traditional way of investing. It is based on the theory that even if the short-term movement of the price of an asset may not be in line with economic fundamentals, eventually the price of the assets will follow the economic numbers. Fundamental analysis takes into account such things as interest rates and economic reports.

Economic indicators are pieces of data from important economic reports. Most of the economic indicators are published by government agencies or select private groups. In Chapter 6, we will learn little bit more about these economic reports and how to use the available tools to make trading decisions.

Technical Analysis

Technical analysis follows from what is called the efficient market theory, where it is assumed that all information about a particular asset is known to everyone interested in that asset. A fundamental principle of technical analysis is that a market's price reflects all relevant information, so this analysis looks at the history of an asset's trading pattern rather than external drivers, such as economic, fundamental, and news events. Therefore, price action tends to repeat itself due to investors collectively tending towards patterned behaviour; hence, technical analysis focuses on identifiable trends and conditions.

As mentioned in Chapter 1, the trading method described in this book does not require traders to learn everything about fundamental analysis but just one aspect of it that might influence the decision in entering into a trade. The key to the trading method described in this book is technical analysis, and I have devoted a significant portion of this book in explaining the technical analysis required to trade binary options.

The technical analysis starts with a proper charting tool—in this case, candlestick charts. This is followed by a number of other tools that help you refine your forecast using other tools on the candlestick charts. So I suggest, devote as much time as required to understand what technical analysis is and also how to become reasonably confident in doing your own technical analysis using the tools recommended in the following chapters and in making trading decisions.

— **End of Chapter 4** —

CHAPTER 5

Technical Analysis: Candlestick Charting

Irrespective of whatever or whenever you trade in financial markets in future, learning to understand candlestick charting will be a great asset to you. This is one tool that I personally respect very much as the panacea for any kind of trading with any asset in any financial market.

Let us first look at various other charts available to traders so that you have an idea of why I am recommending the candlestick chart as your trading tool. I am reproducing three different charts so that you can get an idea of the possible ways an asset price is displayed against time.

Figure 1 shows a line graph typically available in newspapers or other journals when describing any asset in financial markets, be it share price of a popular company or price of gold or the share market index of your country. As obvious from the nature of the chart, it is good for assessing the historical price movement over time and nothing else. As a trader, this information is good to have but provides no information on what is going on in the market and what might result in the next few minutes or hours or days.

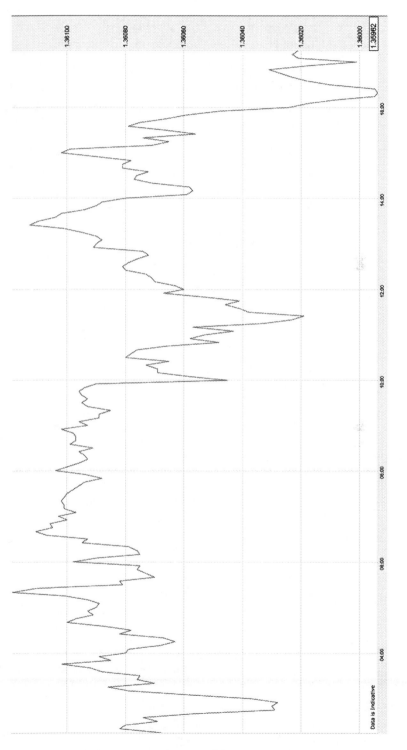

Figure 1: Line graph of a financial asset

Figure 2 shows what is called an OHLC chart. OHLC stands for open, high, low, and close. These charts show the opening, closing, high, and low prices of an asset in a given time frame. This is significant improvement compared to the line graph as we can get little more information than the line graph. Many traders do use it to read the market a little better. As seen in these OHLC charts, each time frame has one vertical line with two small horizontal lines protruding on either side of the vertical line. The small line on the left is the opening price in that time frame, the one on the right is the closing price, and the length of the vertical line is the range of price movement in that time frame.

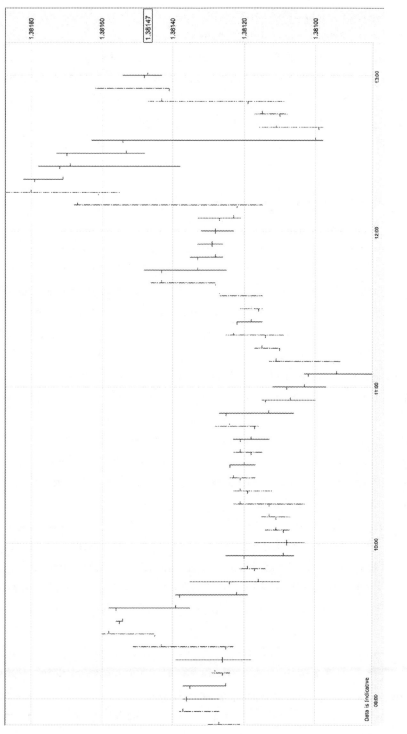

Figure 2: OHLC chart of an asset.

As obvious from the two chart types discussed above, they do not quite provide the information or the information is not substantial enough for us to make trading decisions. A definitely better option is the candlestick chart. Please pay particular attention to the sections below for better understanding of the candlestick chart and its various features so that you can become proficient enough to read a chart and make suitable assessment of the asset's future price movements.

History of Candlestick Charts

First, I will give a brief history of candlestick charts, and then we will go further into the details of it. Please note that candlestick charting is a very vast subject, and there are several outstanding books on this subject alone (please refer to the Further Reading section). To discuss all aspects of candlestick charting in one chapter is impractical and irrelevant, so I will attempt to neatly summarize only those aspects of the candlestick charting that is most important for the type of trading I am advocating in the following sections.

Japanese are believed to be the first to use technical analysis to trade rice futures in the sixteenth century. A Japanese man by the name of Homma, who traded the commodities futures markets in the seventeenth century, discovered that the markets are strongly influenced by traders' emotions, apart from the forces of supply and demand. Homma wanted to capture these emotions in the form of a chart as he realized that he could benefit from understanding the emotions and that it could help him predict the future prices.

Homma understood that there could be a vast difference between value and price of rice because of the emotions involved. This difference between value and price is as valid today with stocks and bonds and futures as it was with rice in Japan centuries ago. The principles established by Homma in measuring market emotions in a stock are the basis for the candlestick chart analysis.

In modern times, two individuals by the name of Steve Nison and Greg Morris introduced candlestick charting to the Western world in 1990s. Subsequently, Steve Nison's book *Japanese Candlestick Charting Techniques*, which was published in 1991, gave the traders in the Western world a great insight into candlestick charting and the practical techniques of how the candlestick chart can be used in a variety of trading environments. Over the years, candlestick charting has grown in popularity and use as more and more traders started using candlestick charts. Candlestick charts can be a valuable tool in the technician's toolbox as it gives insight into current investor sentiment, allowing for the determination of short-term trends and tops and bottoms.

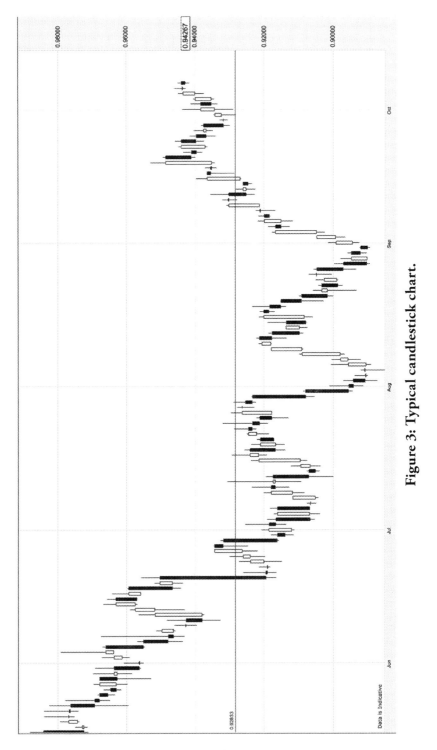

Figure 3: Typical candlestick chart.

Candlestick Charts for Beginners

A typical candlestick chart is shown in Figure 3. As obvious from the chart, it is visually more pleasing than the OHLC chart although it provides the same information.

Like all other charts, a candlestick chart shows the history of how price in the market—equity or commodity or bond or forex—has moved over time. Unlike a regular candle we use at home, which has a wick at the top, each candle in a candlestick chart has a wick at either end usually. There may be candles in a chart which may not have any wick at all or wick at one end only; please see various types of candles in the chart in Figure 3.

Prices move because of supply and demand in the market. If there are more buyers than sellers, prices would go up and vice versa. In trading terminology, buyers are called bulls as they aim to make a profit from the market by buying an asset and selling it when prices move higher. So the buyers' sentiment is that price will go higher and higher and hence the term *bullish*. On the contrary, sellers are called bears as they aim to make a profit from a falling market by selling an asset first and then buying it back when the price falls. So the seller's sentiment is that the price of an asset will fall and will perhaps continue to fall. From bulls and bears come the other two terms—*bullish* and *bearish*.

Buyers and sellers in the market range from people like you and me (who can be classified as speculators) to institutional buyers (such as banks and financial institutions) or commodities producers and commodities users. We could be speculators, as a matter of fact, most likely we are as we look to take advantage from price movements without having any intention to ever own anything in the market. Or in simple terms, with the advent of electronic trading, you can buy an asset in any market with the intention to sell it when the price goes up and make a profit in the process. Large financial institutions also do the same thing. The only difference is that speculators like us may be investing a few hundred dollars whereas large financial institutions will invest millions or even billions of dollars of their own cash or fundraised through their investment banking business.

Large buy-or-sell orders in any market have significant effects on the price movement. These large buy-or-sell orders create a market sentiment which is either short term or long term. All these sentiments are reflected in the candlestick chart in the form of various patterns that such price movements create.

Because we are retail traders and trade in small amounts, which has no effect on the price movements in the market, we can look to understand the sentiments in the market and trade with it. So the challenge is to understand the sentiment and make our decisions based on whether or not price is going up or down in a chosen time frame.

Each candle tells you how the price has moved during a particular period of time—say, from 10 a.m. till 11 a.m., in which case the candlestick chart will be said to be of one-hour time frame. This means that the candlestick which started at 10 a.m. will have captured all the price movements during that hour. Similarly, candlestick charts could be any time frame that you choose, depending upon your style of trading. We will go into details of our preferred time frame for this type of trading in the subsequent chapters. I will deal with two different time frames; details will follow soon.

In the rest of the book, the words *candle* and *candlestick* will be used interchangeably but will mean the same thing. Similarly, the words *asset* and *security* will also be used interchangeably and will mean the same thing.

Each candle can be an increasing candle, which is shown in *white* on the right in Figure 4, or a decreasing candle, which is shown in *black* on the left. There are no hard and fast rules about the colour of the candles in a candlestick chart. In most cases, you may configure your chart to have a colour of your choice for the increasing candle and decreasing candle. The common practice is to use green or blue for the increasing candle and red or orange for the decreasing candle. The contrasting colours give traders an immediate visual clue of whether the price of the asset had increased or decreased in that time frame. Rising candle is the one where the price at close of the candle (at 11 a.m.) is higher than the price at which the candle started (at 10 a.m.), using the example one-hour time frame we have used. Similarly, a falling candle is the one where the price at the close of one hour is lower than the price at the opening of the hour. Figure 4 will clarify the points made here.

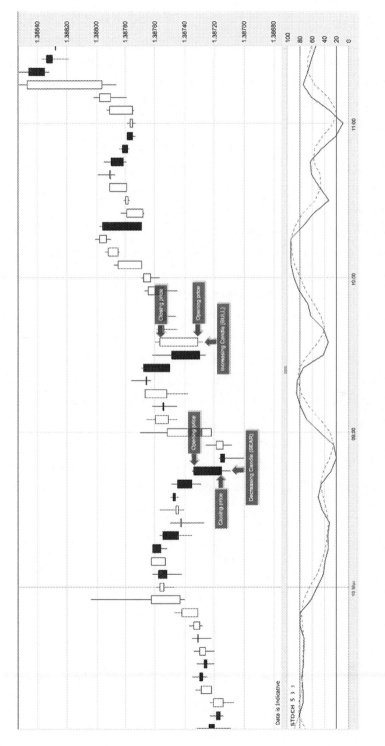

Figure 4: Candlestick description decreasing (*bear*) on the left and increasing (*bull*) on the right.

As stated above, each candlestick has a body and wick at both ends or at either end. They are also called shadows. Various parameters of a candle—such as size of the body, size of the shadow, position of the wick—give the trader an indication of the sentiment in the market. We as traders will look to make an assessment of the sentiments in the market and exploit these sentiments to make a decision about the possible movement of the price in the following time frames. Stated in other words, we are going to make a prediction on whether the following few candles in the candlestick chart is going to be such that the value of the asset is going to be above or below the current value based on a few set-up indications including the previous candle or last few candles.

In this chapter, we are going to have a look at individual candlesticks and various candlestick formations in little more detail. These formations are very critical as they convey additional information compared to single candlesticks, and they could add tremendous value to your trading results.

Let's first look at the single-candlestick formations as in our style of trading we are likely to use single-candlestick formation more often. As you have noticed in this section, the length of shadows and size of the body can give us indications of the sentiment in the market as we look to exploit the sentiment. In the following section, we are going to look at the single-candlestick formations and their features and also what their emotional indications are.

Please note that in all the candlestick chart examples and the related figures, I have shown you full charts with specific candlestick in discussion clearly identified so that you get an understanding of the context and better clarity of how and when such candlesticks are formed in a live chart.

Single-Candlestick Formations

Doji Candlestick

Physical feature

A doji in a candlestick chart looks like a single vertical line caused by the opening price of the asset being the same as the closing price. The candle has no body, just wicks or shadows on both sides of a non-existent body.

Emotional feature

Doji in Japanese literally means 'clumsy' or 'clueless'. In trading psychology, it is a sign of indecisiveness. Buyers and sellers in the markets are about in equilibrium, and the closing price of the market is the same as the opening price within a given time frame.

A doji represents equilibrium between supply and demand, a tug of war that neither the bulls (buyers) nor bears (sellers) are winning. In the case of an uptrend, the bulls have, by definition, won previous battles since prices have moved higher. Now, the outcome of the latest skirmish is in doubt. After a long downtrend, the opposite is true. The bears have been victorious in previous battles, forcing prices down. Now the bulls have found the courage to buy, and the tide may be ready to turn.

Types of doji candles

There are four types of doji candlesticks: common doji, long-legged doji, dragonfly doji, and gravestone doji. All dojis are marked by the fact that prices opened and closed at the same level. If prices close very close to the same level (so that no real body is visible or the real body is very small), then that candle can also be interpreted as a doji.

Common Doji

A common doji, also called a doji star, has a relatively small price movement range compared to the candles immediately preceding and following the doji candle. Figure 5 shows two doji candles in short succession in one chart. A common doji also has almost equal length of wick on both sides. Various doji candles are differentiated by the length of wicks on both sides or on either side of the closing/opening price as described in the following sections.

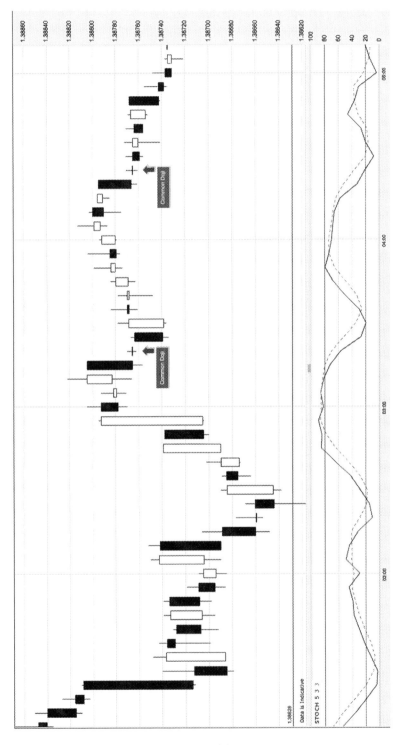

Figure 5: A common doji in a candlestick chart.

Long-Legged Doji

A long-legged doji is a type of candlestick formation where the opening and closing prices are nearly equal despite a lot of price movement throughout the trading period. This candlestick is often used to signal indecision about the future direction of the underlying asset. The key difference between long-legged doji and common doji is that the former has a much longer trading range compared to the latter. In other words, a long-legged doji has much longer wicks on both sides compared to a common doji. The long-legged doji is composed of long upper and lower shadows. Throughout the time period, the price moved up and down dramatically before it closed at or very near the opening price. This reflects the great indecision that exists between the bulls and the bears.

Similar to the common doji, long-legged doji candles are deemed to be the most significant when they occur during a strong uptrend or downtrend. The long-legged doji suggests that the forces of supply and demand are nearing equilibrium and that a shift in the direction of the trend may be coming.

Please see Figure 6 for example of long-legged doji in a candlestick chart.

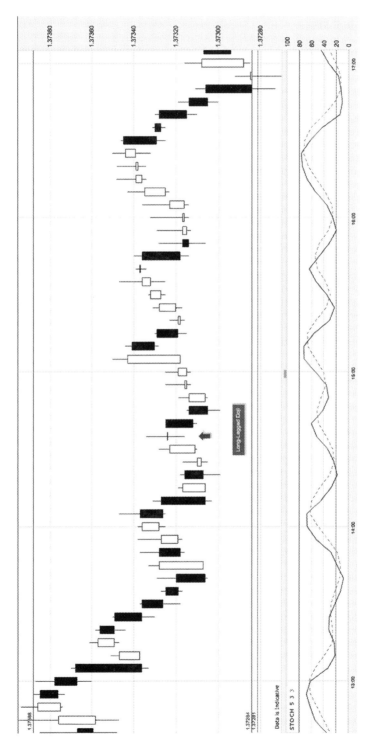

Figure 6: Typical long-legged doji.

Gravestone Doji

A gravestone doji is a type of candlestick pattern that is formed when the opening and closing prices of the underlying asset are equal and occur at the lower end of the price. The long upper shadow suggests that the buying pressure during the period of time was countered by the sellers and that the forces of supply and demand are nearing a balance. This pattern is commonly used to suggest that the direction of the trend may be nearing a major turning point.

A gravestone doji pattern is a common reversal pattern used by traders to suggest that a bearish rally or trend is about to reverse. It can also be found at the end of a uptrend, but this version is much rarer.

The gravestone doji is formed when the open and the close occur at the low end of the trading range. The price opens at the low end of the time frame and rallies from there, but by the close, the price is beaten back down to the opening price.

Please see Figure 7 for example of a gravestone doji at the end of a short-term downtrend in a candlestick chart.

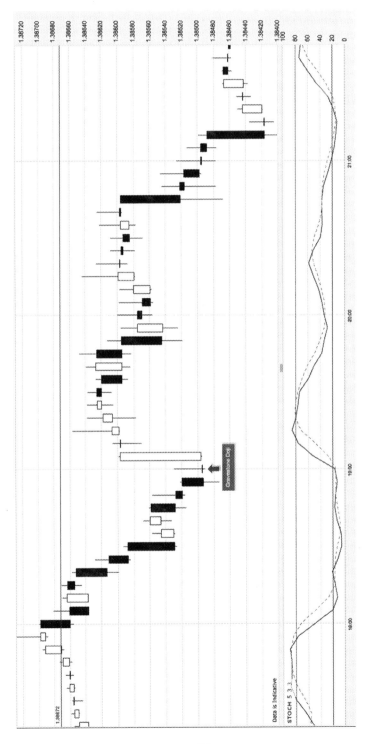

Figure 7: Gravestone doji at the end of a downtrend.

Dragonfly Doji

As with all doji candles, dragonfly doji is a type of candlestick pattern that signals indecision among traders. The pattern is formed when the asset's opening and closing prices are equal and occur at the higher end of the price range. The long lower shadow suggests that the forces of supply and demand are nearing a balance and that the direction of the trend may be nearing a major turning point.

A dragonfly doji pattern is a relatively difficult chart pattern to find, but when it is found in a uptrend, it is often deemed to be a reliable signal that the trend is about to change direction. The close near the time frame's opening price suggests that demand is again starting to outweigh supply.

The dragonfly doji occurs when trading opens, trades lower, then closes at the open price, which is the higher end of the time period. An extensively long shadow on a dragonfly doji at the bottom of a trend is very bullish.

Please see Figure 8 for example of dragonfly doji at the end of the short-term uptrend in a candlestick chart.

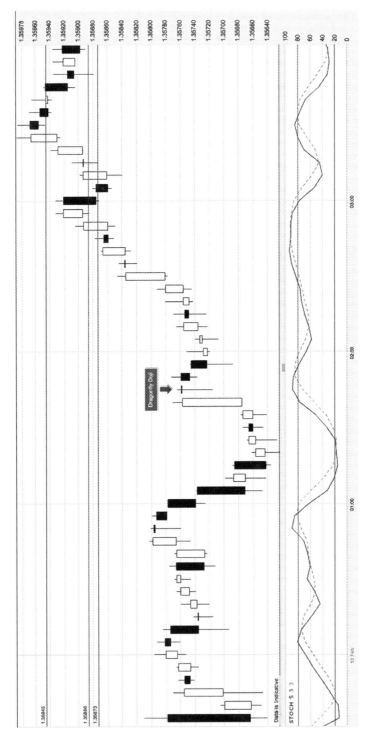

Figure 8: Dragonfly doji at the end of a short uptrend.

Spinning-Top Candlestick

Physical feature

Spinning-top candlestick is a type of candlestick formation where the real body is small despite a wide range of price movement throughout the trading period in a given time frame. This candle is often regarded as neutral and used to signal indecision about the future direction of the underlying asset.

Emotional feature

If a spinning-top formation is found after a prolonged uptrend, it suggests that the bulls are losing interest in the asset and that a reversal may be in the cards. On the other hand, if this formation is found in a downtrend, it suggests that the sellers are losing conviction and that a bottom may be forming. Or in other words, the formation of a spinning-top candle is an indication of possible price reversal.

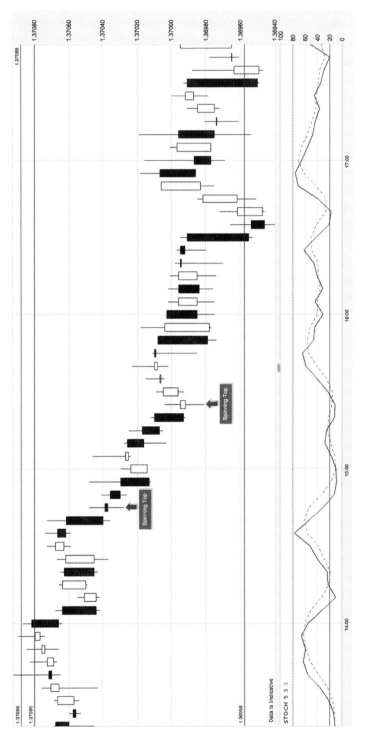

Figure 9: Spinning-top candles during and at the end of a downtrend.

Hammer Candlestick

Physical feature

Hammer candlestick is doubtlessly one of the most visually compelling candles in a candlestick chart as it is easily recognized by the lower shadow protruding to the downside. It is easily identified by the presence of a small body with a shadow at least two times greater than the body. Hammer candles can be found in the charts of almost any asset types, from stocks to indices and to forex candlestick charts. This is the type of candle where lower price in the trading range has been rejected by the market as evident from the longer wick at the bottom. As such, this candle is a type of price rejection candle.

Emotional feature

After a downtrend has been in effect for a few time frames, the sentiment in the market seems to be very bearish. The price opens and starts to trade lower as the bears are still in control. The bulls then step in and start bringing the price back up towards the top of the trading range. This creates a small body with a large lower shadow. This represents that the bears could not maintain control. The long lower shadow now has the bears questioning whether the decline is still intact. A higher open on the next time frame would confirm that the bulls had taken control.

A hammer occurs after an asset price has been declining, possibly suggesting the market is attempting to determine a bottom and the evidence that the bulls started to step in. The colour of the small body is not important, but a bull candle has slightly more bullish implications than the bear body.

Please see Figure 10 for a bear hammer candlestick and Figure 11 for a bull hammer candlestick in live charts.

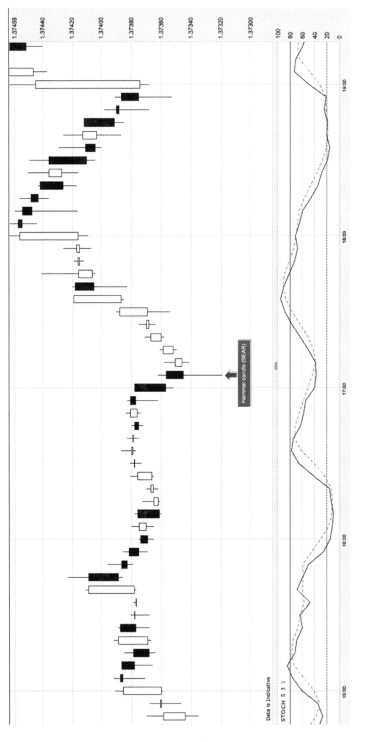

Figure 10: *bear* hammer candlestick.

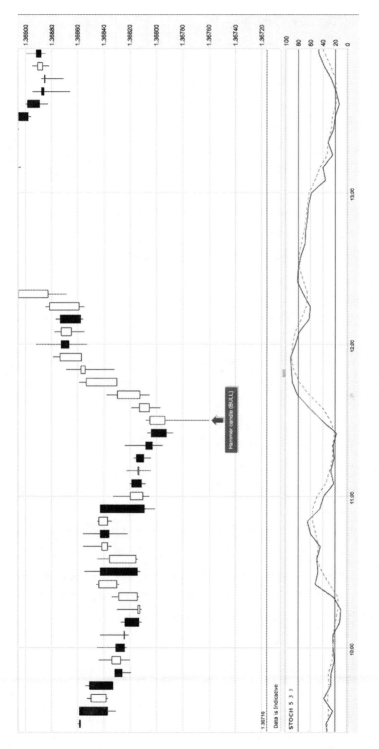

Figure 11: *bull* hammer candlestick.

Hanging-Man Candlestick

Physical feature

Hanging-man candle is another visually compelling single-candlestick formation identified by a long wick at the bottom and a much smaller body, usually less than one-third of the total range of the candle. It is also a type of price rejection candle as it has a much longer wick in the lower side of the body but has a very small or no wick at the upper end. The Japanese named this pattern as such because it looks like a head with the feet dangling down.

The hanging-man candle and hammer candle have the same physical attribute except that a hanging-man candle is usually formed in an uptrend whereas a hammer candle is formed in a downtrend of price.

Emotional Feature

After an uptrend has been in effect for a few time frames, the atmosphere seems to be bullish. The price opens higher in the following time frame but starts to move lower. The bears appear to have taken control. But before the end of the same time frame, the bulls step in and take the price back up to the higher end of the trading range, creating a small body. This makes it look like that the bulls still have control. However, the long lower shadow represents that the sellers had started stepping in at these levels and the price of the asset might move lower in subsequent time frames. Even though the bulls may have been able to keep the price positive during the time frame, the evidence of the selling was apparent.

While formation of a hanging-man candle at the top of an uptrend could be a signal that the price of the asset might fall, it is better validated with a couple of other indicators, such as stochastic oscillator or a resistance line, both of which we are going to learn later in this chapter and the following chapter.

Please see Figure 12 for a chart with a hanging-man candle.

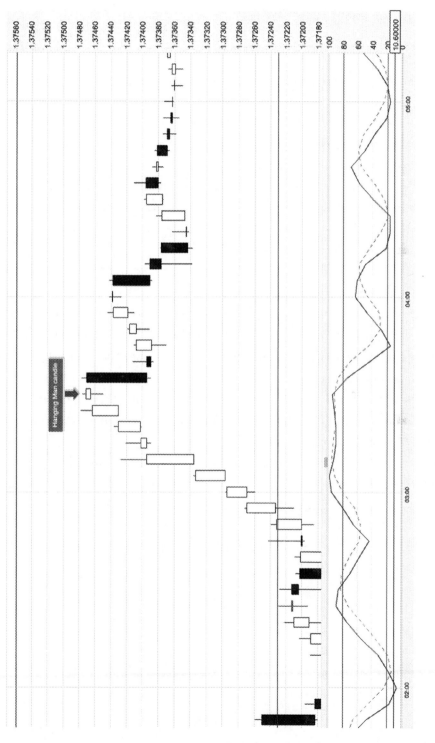

Figure 12: Hanging man candlestick in an uptrend

Shooting-Star Candlestick

Physical feature

The shooting-star candlestick is also a single-candlestick formation. It is easily identified by the presence of a small body with a shadow at least two times greater than the body. It is found at the top of an uptrend. The Japanese named this pattern as such because it looks like a shooting star falling from the sky with the tail trailing after it.

In physical features, shooting-star candle is very similar to the inverted-hammer candle we are about to learn, the only difference being that the candle is named shooting star as it is formed in an uptrend, whereas an inverted-hammer candle is formed in a downtrend.

Emotional feature

After a strong uptrend has been in effect for a reasonably prolonged period of time, the atmosphere seems to be very bullish. The price opens and trades higher as bulls are in control. But before the end of the time frame, the bears step in and take the price back down to the lower end of the trading range, thus creating a small body with a long wick at the top. This might indicate that the bulls are still in control, but the long upper shadow represents that the bears, or sellers, had started stepping in at these price levels, causing the price to move down. Even though the bulls may have been able to keep the price higher than the opening price in that time frame, the evidence of the selling was apparent as the price couldn't be kept at the higher side of the range in the given time frame.

Please see Figure 13 for a candlestick chart with a shooting-star candle.

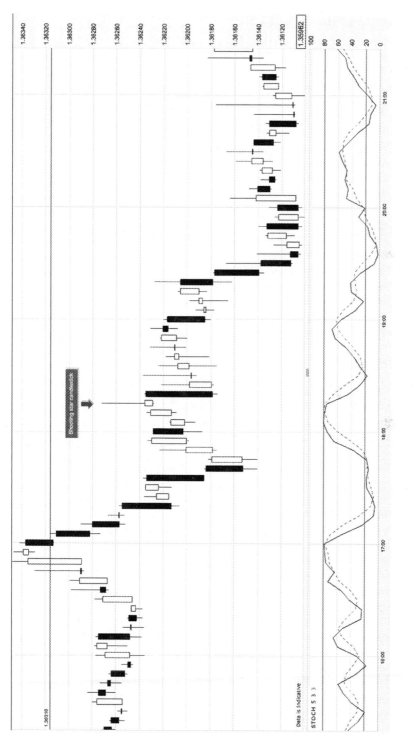

Figure 13: Shooting-star candle at the end of an uptrend.

Inverted-Hammer Candlestick

Physical feature

The inverted-hammer candle is a single-candlestick formation usually found at the bottom of a downtrend. It is also classified as price rejection candle. It is identified as a candle with a smaller body at least two times the size of the body on the upper side but has a very small or no wick below the body. As the name suggests, it is the same as the hammer candle you just learnt, but upside down. Although this is a price rejection candle with higher price rejection in the current time frame, it is an indication of a bullish reversal if supported by the confluence of other indicators, such as stochastic oscillator and support line.

Emotional feature

After a downtrend has been in effect for the last few time frames, the atmosphere appears to be bearish. The price opens and starts to trade higher. The bulls seem to be in control, but they cannot maintain the strength as the momentum seems to be slowly declining. The sellers watching the market step in, and selling pressure increases. With increased sell-off, the price moves down to the lower end of the trading range or even below the opening price in the time frame. The bears are still in control. This movement of price of the asset in the given time frame causes the formation of a candle with a long wick at the top, resembling the shape of an inverted hammer. However, the bulls, or buyers, are also watching to be back in the market after the price has dropped for a while. And this is the signal that the price is expected to go up in the following time frame after the bulls have stepped in.

Please refer to Figure 14 for an inverted hammer candlestick in a live chart.

We have so far discussed single-candlestick formations, which are based on high or low price rejection. These are the keys to our strategy as the rejection of price means that the price of the asset is expected to move in the opposite direction or in the same direction at which the price was rejected.

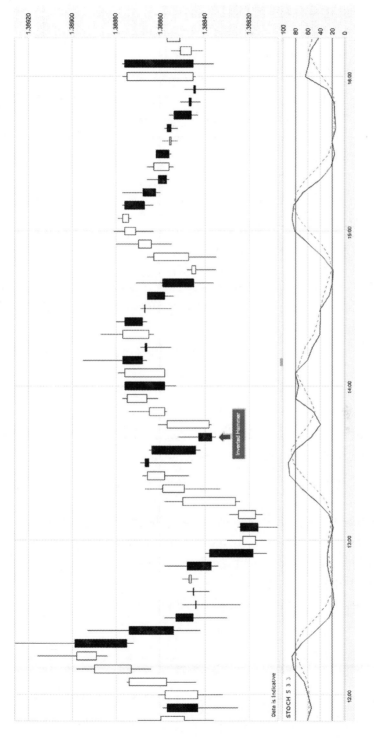

Figure 14: Inverted-hammer candle in a candlestick chart.

Multiple-Candlestick Formations

We are going to discuss a couple of multiple-candlestick formations in this section which are relevant to the trading method to be described later in this book. There is a range of candlestick formations that traders use when trading other assets in a much longer time frame, such as traders trading stocks and deciding to buy and hold it over a few days. But for now, we are going to focus on only a couple of those that are useful for the short-term trading method discussed in this book.

Bullish Engulfing Candlestick

Physical feature

A bullish engulfing candle is a two-candle formation in a candlestick chart in which a *bull* candle is formed immediately after a *bear* candle, the body of the *bull* candle being bigger than the body of the *bear* candle and completely covering the *bear* candle. Usually, such a candle formation is found during a downtrend.

Emotional feature

A bullish engulfing candle formation is considered one of the major signals of bullish reversal or indication of price moving upwards in the following time frames. After a downtrend has been in effect, the price opens lower than where it closed in the previous time frame. Before the close of the current time frame, the buyers have taken over and moved the price above where it opened in the previous time frame. The bullish engulfing pattern represents a change in investor sentiment towards bullish. The emotional psychology of the trend has now been altered.

Please see Figure 15 for an example of a bullish engulfing candle formation.

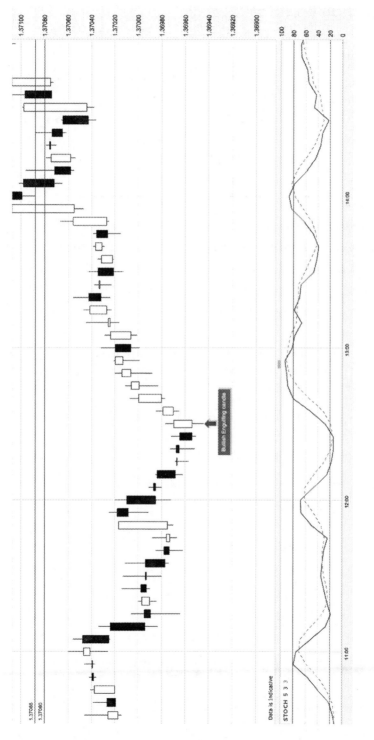

Figure 15: Bullish engulfing candle at the end of a downtrend.

Bearish Engulfing Candlestick

Physical feature

The bearish engulfing candlestick formation is just the opposite of the bullish engulfing candle formation except that the candle in question is a *bear* candle and it is formed in an uptrend. In bearish candlestick formation, the *bear* candle is larger in body than the *bull* candle so that the candle is fully covered by the body of the *bear* candle.

Emotional feature

After an uptrend has been in effect for a period of time, the price opens higher in the current time frame than where it closed in the previous time frame. Before the end of the current time frame, the bears, or sellers, have taken over and moved the price below where it opened the day before. The bearish engulfing pattern represents a complete change in investor sentiment from bullish to bearish as bears enter the market and sell off the asset to push the price down to an even lower level. In an uptrend, a bearish engulfing candle is usually followed by further sell-off so that the price of the asset keeps falling till bulls step in to reverse the trend.

Please see Figure 16 for an example of the bearish candlestick formation.

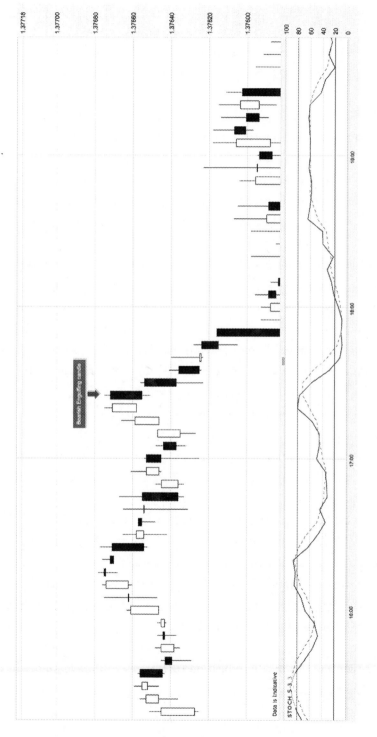

Figure 16: Bearish engulfing candle at the end of an uptrend.

All the single- and double-candlestick formations discussed in this chapter give us an immediate view about the possible movement of the price in the next time frame. There are more multiple-candle patterns—such as piercing pattern, dark cloud, bullish harami, bearish harami, morning star, evening star, and kicker signals—which are formed by a combination of two or three candles. Those candlestick patterns are also very important for traders when trading using much larger time frames, such as daily or weekly charts. Since we are working on a style of trading which involves a much shorter time frame, I am not going to spend time on those multiple-candle patterns, but interested readers may refer to the Further Reading section for more on the subject.

Here is a summary of the candlestick formations we have discussed so far:

1. Doji candle: it is an indication of indecisiveness in the market and possible reversal of price, depending upon the type of doji candle.
2. Spinning-top candle: it is found in an uptrend or downtrend and is an indication of a possible reversal of price—meaning prices are likely to go up if in a downtrend or down if the candle is found in an uptrend.
3. Hammer candle: when there is a formation of a hammer candle in a downtrend where lower prices were rejected, it is expected that the price of the asset will move higher
4. Shooting-star candle: when there is a formation of a shooting-star candle in an uptrend where higher prices have been rejected, it is expected that the price of the asset will move lower in the following timeframe.
5. Inverted-hammer candle: when there is a formation of an inverted-hammer candle in a downtrend where the higher prices have been rejected, the price is expected to move higher.
6. Hanging-man candle: when there is a formation of a hanging-man candle where lower prices have been rejected, it is expected that the price of the asset will move lower.
7. Bullish engulfing candle: formation of a bullish engulfing candle in a downtrend is a likely indication that prices will move higher in the following time frame.

8. Bearish engulfing candle: formation of a bearish engulfing candle in an uptrend is a likely indication that the prices will move lower in the following time frame.

In Chapter 9 of this book, we are going to learn to use candlesticks along with other indicators to make our decision to enter a trade.

— **End of Chapter 5** —

CHAPTER 6
Tools of the Trade

In this section, I am going to talk about all the tools you need to start your trading career for trading binary options. Some of the tools mentioned here are quite universal as you will need these even if you decide to trade other instruments in a different financial market. But for now, please note that each of these tools are very critical for you so that you can read the market in short term and take a position or enter into a trade based on your interpretation of the price movement using the tools described in this chapter.

Tool No. 1: Technical Indicators

Technical indicators, or simply called indicators, are additional graphs or charts which are usually superimposed on a candlestick chart. They provide additional information on the market condition by calculating various parameters from the main price action in the candlestick chart. An indicator is a series of data points that are derived by applying a formula to the price data of an asset. Price data could be any combination of the open, high, low, or close over a period of time. Some indicators may use only the closing prices while others incorporate volume and open interest into their formulas. The price data is entered into the formula, and a data point is produced.

For example, the average of three closing prices is one data point (41 + 43 + 43) / 3 = 42.33). However, one data point does not offer much information and does not make an indicator. A series of data points over a period of time is required to create valid reference points to enable analysis. By creating a time series of data points, a comparison can be made between present and past levels. For analysis purposes, technical indicators are usually shown in a graphical form above or below an asset's price chart. Once shown in graphical form, an indicator can then be compared with the corresponding price chart of the security. Sometimes indicators are plotted on top of the price plot for a more direct comparison.

There is a range of indicators that technical analysts use, and a discussion on the whole range will consume an entire book. Some of the most popular indicators are EMA (exponential moving average), SMA (simple moving average), MACD (moving average convergence/divergence), and RSI (relative strength index). I will draw your attention to only a couple of those that are critical to making the decision for trading binary options, but please note that indicators are generally lagging, meaning that they follow the price action and are commonly referred to as trend-following indicators. Rarely, if ever, will these indicators lead the price of an asset. There are numerous books on various indicators and their uses in various types of trading. Please refer to the Further Reading section for more details. But for the purpose of simplicity, I am going to mention just two very popular indicators below. We will, however, be using one of these two indicators in our trading decisions.

A technical indicator offers a different perspective from which to analyze the price action. Some, such as moving averages, are derived from simple formulas, and the mechanics are relatively easy to understand. Others, such as the stochastic oscillator, have complex formulas and require more study for us to fully understand and appreciate. Regardless of the complexity of the formula, technical indicators can provide a unique perspective on the strength and direction of the underlying price action.

Simple Moving Average

A simple moving average is an indicator that calculates the average price of an asset over a specified number of periods. If the asset is exceptionally volatile, then a moving average will help to smooth the data. A moving average filters out random noise and offers a smoother perspective of the price action. As an example is when an instrument displays a lot of volatility and an analyst may have difficulty discerning a trend. By applying a ten-day simple moving average to the price action, random fluctuations are smoothed to make it easier to identify a trend.

Please see Figure 17 for simple moving average indicator added to a candlestick chart. As evident from Figure 17, the random fluctuations of the price movement in the candlestick chart has been smoothened to a wavy line running across the chart representing the rolling average of the prices based on certain the number of price points of the asset that you may choose. In this example in Figure 17, the moving average indicator is based on 100 periods.

Many traders use multiple simple moving average indicators on the same chart with different periods such as 20, 50 and 100 or 5, 10 and 50 to understand price movement trend and to make a decision to buy or sell.

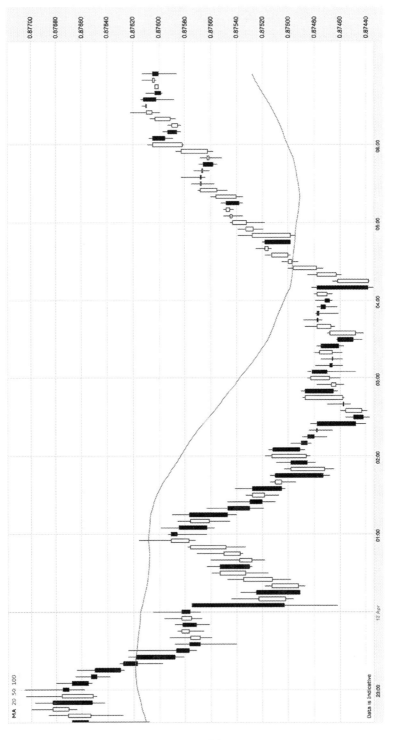

Figure 17: Simple moving average added to a candlestick chart.

Stochastic Oscillator

The stochastic oscillator, a very popular indicator among traders, developed by Dr. George Lane, is based on the premise that prices tend to close near their high during an upward trading market and that prices tend to close near their low during a downward trading market. In other words, stochastic oscillator is a momentum indicator as it helps determine when the price of an asset is about to change direction. It does this by giving signals on whether an asset is overbought or oversold.

The Stochastic Oscillator is displayed as two lines. The main line is called "%K." The second line, called "%D," is a moving average of %K. The %K line is usually displayed as a solid line and the %D line is usually displayed as a dotted line.

The mathematical equation used to calculate the %K is as follows:

$$\%K = 100[(C - L1)/(H1 - L1)]$$

Where

C is the latest closing price of the asset,
L1 is the lowest price traded during previous %K periods, and
H1 is the highest price traded during the same period

As you have noticed, the Stochastic Oscillator requires three variables to plot the indicator on your chart, those are:

%K periods: this is the number of time periods used in the stochastic calculation.
%K slowing periods: this value controls the internal smoothing of %K. A value of 1 is considered a fast stochastic; a value of 3 is considered a slow stochastic.
%D Periods: this is the number of time periods used when calculating a moving average of %K. The moving average is called "%D" and is usually displayed as a dotted line on top of %K.

Please see Figure 18 for a candlestick chart with stochastic indicator added. I have purposefully included the stochastic indicator in most of the previous candlestick chart examples as I wanted you to be asking what those wavy lines under the charts were. And now you know what those lines were. Despite of the indicator being over 50 years old, it still remains as one of the most popular indicators used by traders all over the world.

In Figure 18, the stochastic oscillator uses a %K period of 5, %K slowing period of 3 and %D period of 3. Some traders use 14,3,3 setting for the indicator while some other traders use a even different setting. The obvious difference between %K period of 5 and 14 is that a higher %K period setting makes the indicator look smoother than a lower setting of the %K period. For some traders, this is a way to eliminate false indication of the overbought or oversold signal.

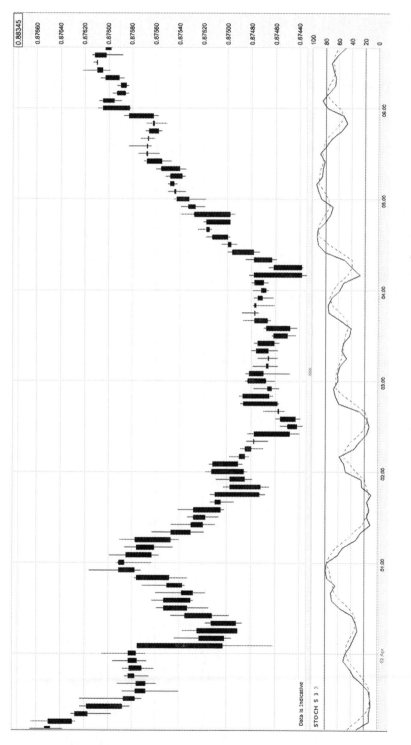

Figure 18: Stochastic oscillator indicator added to a chart.

Tool No. 2: Support and Resistance

Take a look at the candlestick chart and see whether you can find any pattern in it or whether it's just random. It might look random in some instances, but look at it from a few other perspectives. For example, increase the time period of display from a few hours to 24 hours or maybe a few days.

When you open the candlestick chart, there are a few options that you can play with—for example, adjusting the candlestick period. That's the time it takes to form each candle. For the trading method described in this book, we will use a 5-minute candle or a 15-minute candle. Let's start with a 5-minute candle.

With a 5-minute candle, you can realistically display between 10 to 12 hours' worth of charts on a desktop. Let's try to squeeze more number of hours on the display by zooming out. You might like to try to display, say, 24 hours' worth of candlestick on the chart.

Do you see anything different from the original setting? My feeling is that you might have noticed something more. Do you see that during that time period, the price bounced off some fixed number a few times? See Figure 19 for an illustration of what I mean.

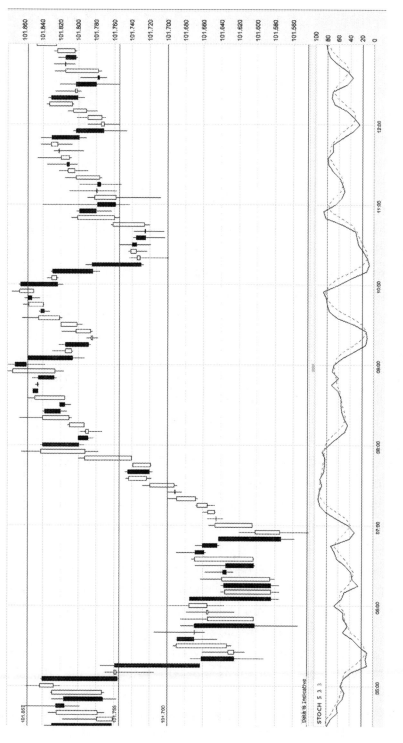

Figure 19: USDJPY five-minute chart.

Did you notice that in the candlestick chart at Figure 19, the asset price bounced at around 101.700 a few times, and then it went up to a higher number?

Similarly, did you also notice that the prices could not go above 101.870 and bounced off from that level two times so far? The price may attempt to go there again and might bounce off again as it did the last couple of times, or it might pierce through and go to another higher level.

For the purpose of explaining the points here, let's put some names used by traders all over the world, and it will also help us make the discussion easier. The ongoing battle between the bulls and the bears or the struggle between buyers (demand) and sellers (supply) is revealed by the prices of an asset that seldom moves above or below certain levels. The line at which the price bounced back to move higher is called *support*. Similarly, the line at which the price bounced to move lower is called *resistance*.

Why does this happen? This happens because, at those price levels, the strength of buyers and numbers are about equal, and hence, market equilibrium is reached. Once the equilibrium is reached, the price may travel in one of the two directions. It either moves in the opposite direction (or bounces off from that equilibrium price) or continues to travel in the same direction as the one it did to get to the equilibrium position.

Support and resistance levels are the levels at which a lot of traders are willing to buy the asset (in the case of a support) or sell it (in the case of resistance). When these trend lines are broken, the supply and demand and the psychology behind the asset's price movements are thought to have shifted, in which case new levels of support and resistance will likely be established.

Round Numbers and Support and Resistance

One type of universal support and resistance that tends to be seen across a large number of securities is round numbers. Round numbers—like 10, 20, 35, 50, 100, and 1,000—tend be important in support and resistance levels because they often represent the major psychological turning points at which many traders will make buy or sell decisions. In currency market, the round numbers could be in form of number of zeros at the end of the decimal point in price level; more the number of zeros, the stronger the support or resistance.

For example, in this case the round number support or resistance could be at 101.900, 101.800, 101.500 and so on or at 102.000, 103.000 etc.

Buyers will often purchase large amounts of stock once the price starts to fall towards a major round number, such as $50, which makes it more difficult for shares to fall below the level. On the other hand, sellers start to sell off a stock as it moves towards a round-number peak, making it difficult to move past this upper level as well. It is the increased buying and selling pressure at these levels that makes them important points of support and resistance and, in many cases, major psychological points as well.

Role Reversal: Support Becomes Resistance

Once a resistance or support level is broken, its role may be reversed. If the price falls below a support level, that level will become resistance. If the price rises above a resistance level, it will often become support. As the price moves past a level of support or resistance, it is thought that the supply and demand have shifted, causing the breached level to reverse its role. For a true reversal to occur, however, it is important that the price makes a strong move through either the support or resistance.

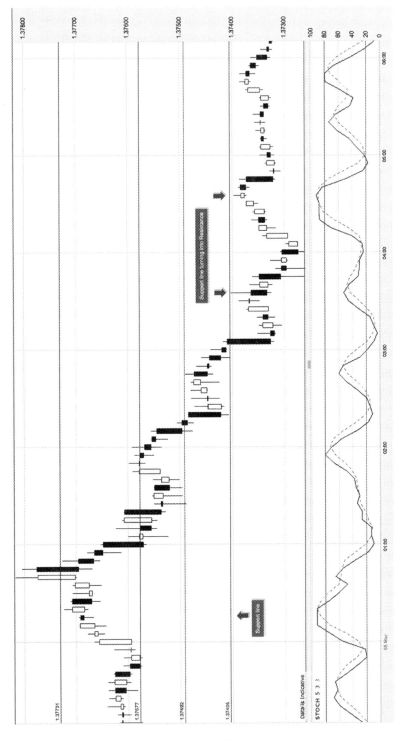

Figure 20: Support line can turn into resistance.

For example, as you can see in Figure 20, a previous support line at price level of 1.37405 was breached at around 03:05 hours. After that the support level turned into a resistance level as the price failed to go above the 1.37405 level on three occasions.

Many traders who begin using technical analysis find this concept hard to believe and don't realize that this phenomenon occurs rather frequently—almost with all kind of assets in a financial market.

In almost every case, an asset will have both a level of support and a level of resistance and will trade in this range as it bounces between these levels. This is most often seen when an asset is trading in a generally sideways manner as the price moves through successive peaks and troughs, testing resistance and support levels.

The Importance of Support and Resistance

The importance of support and resistance lines can not be overstated as traders, large or small, around the world take notice of the various price levels of an asset and make their trading decisions based on those levels. So, to an extent, this is a self full-filling prophecy. You now would have got a fairly good understanding of why price of an asset bounces from specific levels. We are going to use this knowledge in making decisions when entering into a trade.

However, please bear in mind few points: if the price has bounced from a level few times in past, does it mean that it will always bounce from the same level again and again? Perhaps not, the reason being, at some point of time the price of the asset will pierce through that support or resistance level and it will either retrace back ignoring that level or the role of the level will be reversed, meaning if it was a support level, it will become a resistance level and vice versa.

Now the obvious question is how would you know what is the likelihood of price to bounce back from a support or resistance level? My suggestion is to observe how many times in past has this level been respected, meaning the price did bounce off the level. If price had bounced couple of times, then there is a stronger chance that the level will be respected and the price will bounce off again. My observation is that, generally the price does not bounce of more than two to three times from the same level. So watch out. Secondly, look for other indicators such as stochastic oscillator. The %K and %D lines of the oscillator at 20 or less indicates oversold condition and hence strong chances of the price to bounce off a support line. Similarly, if the %K and %D lines are above 80 or more, indicating overbought condition, the chances are that the price will bounce off the resistance line.

This is the key learning that we are about to use in our trading method, of course along with few other conditions. So, whenever you are about to use a candlestick chart, one of the first things you would like to do is to identify the key support and resistance levels. Identifying the support and resistance levels can be easy as described so far or difficult as some traders make it out. There are vast authoritative articles and books on the subject, one mentioned in the Further Reading section. But follow the KISS principle, it works.

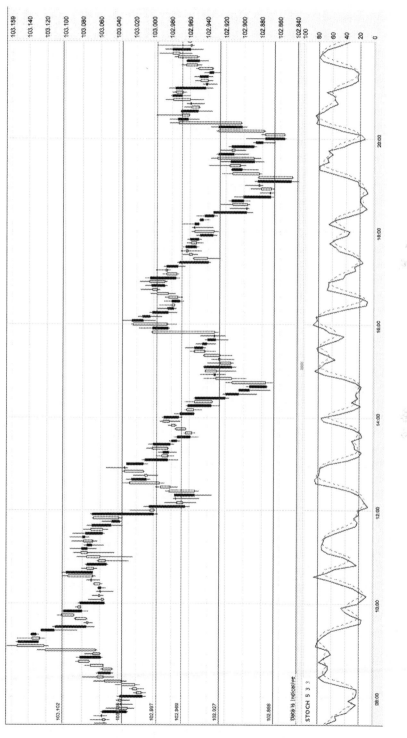

Figure 21: Draw as many lines as required for support and resistance.

Try to draw as many lines as required so that each and every support and resistance line is marked on your chart. It will be obvious from those lines that support or resistance may sometimes be an area in the chart rather than lines. Either way, you will need to be aware of the lines or the areas from which the asset prices might bounce. This, coupled with two other indicators, is our key to enter into a trade as you will learn shortly in the following chapters.

Tool No. 3: Broker

You might be wondering why I have listed the broker as a tool. This is simply because you need to be with a good broker that is not only reliable but also provides you with all the resources that you need to trade an instrument of your choice in the financial market.

Broker is a business entity or an organization that facilitate trading through various stock exchanges or financial markets for retail or institutional traders. They also provide data feed for various financial markets through a variety of methods, some online and some via dedicated charting programmes. But in simple terms, a broker is needed for you to place a trade in the financial market and, in exchange, collects commission from you and sometimes spread, depending on the type of market you are trading.

There are plenty of brokers around the world. Some are very well known, such as Charles Schwab, TD Ameritrade, E*TRADE, Scottrade, while some are relatively obscure and little known. One has to be very cautious in choosing the right broker for the type of trading one is engaged in. In some cases, there are brokers who only offer a specific type or types of products for trade while there are brokers who offer a range of products. Brokers operating in multiple countries may also offer certain types of products in one country and not in the other. For example, IG Markets, known as a global leader in CFD trading, do not offer CFD trading in USA as CFD trading is not allowed in USA, but IG Markets offer to trade CFDs in UK, Europe, and Australia. FXCM, on the other hand, is a dedicated forex broker and provides almost similar types of product offerings in all countries where it operates, and those include forex trading, trading of equity indices, and some commodities such as gold, silver, and platinum.

One of the key concerns about brokers is that there is mushrooming of brokers around the world, making it hard to choose. Depending upon the trading access to financial markets offered by brokers, those brokers are supposed to be regulated by the country's own financial regulators and/or international regulators apart from the rules and regulations enforced by the financial market itself. Some of the brokers operate in relatively loosely regulated regimes, making it hard to make a decision in their favour for trading with them. With the advent of forex trading and binary options, there are many new brokers around the world, some of those with doubtful credentials. I do not want to use the word *doubtful* loosely here because in my experience, there are reasons for one to be suspicious of the intentions of those brokers.

The suspicion arises from two main sources. Firstly, the brokers in question generally offer to trade in forex markets or trade binary options; the latter would be on forex pairs or large market cap US and European shares. As mentioned before, forex are not traded in highly regulated stock exchanges but by large banks. These banks collectively set their conversion rate depending on supply and demand of various currencies at anytime during the trading time, and those prices are then fed to the forex brokers. The prices are in the form of bid and ask price, and the forex brokers then add their own mark-up or spread to these prices and present the final bid and ask price to the trader.

Since most forex brokers earn their money from the bid and ask spread only (they do not usually charge any round-trip commission—one for the opening trade and the other for the closing for straight forward currency trading), those brokers retain the ability to control trades by manipulating those spreads. There are no regulations to control those spreads. The only regulation that applies in those cases are the ones that relates to the safety of the trader's fund with the broker as every trader will be required to fund their account before trading. In the event of a broker going belly up, a trader's fund should be returned to the trader as per the regulation of the country in which the broker is registered.

I am listing below a few brokers that I think you could use for the reasons mentioned above. In addition, these brokers provide a platform which I find very easy to use and suited well for beginners. Please read the disclaimer at the beginning of this book.

Option 1: IG Markets

IG Markets, as mentioned before, is one of the largest CFD providers in the world. IG offers to trade binary options through a few different product classes. Those are listed as binaries. But what we are looking at for trading with IG Markets is called *sprint markets* or *sprint options*. Trading binaries as a product on IG requires a fair bit of learning, whereas the sprint markets is a more customizable version of binary option and much easier to learn and trade.

In sprint options, you can set various parameters, such as asset to trade, expiry time, and the amount of investment. In the following chapters, I will provide details of how to trade sprint markets.

There are also excellent educational resources within the IG Markets' platform and website, which will provide a beginner with information on the platform and on trading various instruments.

One of the best things about the IG Markets' trading platform is that it is Web-based. This means you could log in to the platform from any type of computer using any good browser; no software installation is required. This also means that you could potentially trade from any computer—be it at home or at work or at the airport or in the library—as long as you have a reasonably good browser. I have tested the platform across a few Windows-based browsers—such as Internet Explorer, Firefox, Google Chrome—and Safari on Apple Mac. All these work extremely well, and you can use any one of those combinations to start trading. My personal preference has been Google Chrome on Windows computers and Safari on Apple Mac.

Option 2: Stockpair

Stockpair is one of the new-generation brokers only offering to trade binary options on their Web-based trading platform. Stockpair offers traders to choose from among 100 different asset classes. One of the interesting forms of trading binary options that Stockpair offers is pair options trading, in which a trader is required to predict the relative performance of two different assets under the same class. If the performance of one asset is better than the other and you predicted that correctly, you will receive the payout, else you lose the initial investment. However, for the purpose of our trading, we will focus on simple binary-options trading.

The browser-based platform offered by Stockpair requires no download and can be accessed from any type of computer with an Internet browser. The disadvantage with Stockpair though is that there is no charting platform available within the trading platform, unlike IG Markets. So if you intend to trade with Stockpair, you will have to use a charting platform from another provider. I have discussed one such option in Chapter 9.

Option 3: Core Liquidity Market (CLM)

CLM is a relatively new entity in the binary-options market. The brokerage firm is based in Australia and, as with any company in Australia, conforms to strict ASIC regulation. One of the main reasons for which I have listed CLM as a possible broker for you to consider is the trading platform. CLM is one of the few brokers I am aware of that offers to trade binary options on MT4 platform. MT4, or MetaTrader 4, is a very popular Microsoft Windows–based platform for retail traders around the world, made available by MetaQuotes Software Corp. Many forex brokers offer this platform by default to retail traders whereas some of the mainstream brokers have started offering this platform because of its popularity.

The two broker platforms, such as the ones from IG Markets and Stockpair mentioned above, are Web-based whereas MT4 platform offered by CLM requires you to install software on your computer to trade. You will also need to install an additional piece of software to run concurrently on MT4 to let you trade binary options. But that's a small price to pay for the advantage it offers.

Installing MT4 and the additional software on your computer is pretty much a click-and-run activity and does not require any more expertise than using any other applications on any standard computer. The installation process is fairly simple and seamless. When you sign up for the brokerage, you will be provided detailed instructions on installing the platform software. As such, those details have not been included in this book.

Apart from the differentiation in the trading platform provided by these brokers, they also offer different payouts depending on the asset on which you are trading binary options and also on expiry time. Please check with the broker before signing up. For example, IG Markets offer 81% return on any forex-based binary options and 75% return on equity-index-based binary options irrespective of the expiry time. CLM, on the other hand, offers 80% return on 60-second expiry binary options but only 75% return on expiry above five minutes. A trader may consider various factors to choose their preferred broker, either for the flexibility of the platform or the payout or any other reason. But whichever platform you choose to use, in Chapter 9, I have provided as much details as needed for you to use these platforms, from setting it up for charting to trading for each of these broker's platform.

Tool No. 4: Economic Calendar

One of the most important keys to trading any instrument in any financial market is to be aware of the various planned release of reports on economic data by various government and non-government organizations. All such reports are released as per a calendar, which is often called an economic calendar. This is all the fundamental analysis you would need to do to trade binary options.

You could go to the websites of various publishing entities or watch Bloomberg or CNBC television programmes for these reports. Alternatively, you could visit one of the most popular portals, such as the following, to get the calendar:

1. http://www.forexfactory.com/calendar.php
2. http://www.bloomberg.com/markets/economic-calendar/
3. http://investing.money.msn.com/investments/calendar/economic-data

There are many other sources where you could get the same info. In my trading career so far, I found Forex Factory (www.forexfactory.com) as one of the resources to be invaluable, not because of the economic calendar alone but a range of information that has proved critical for my trading. News section of the Forex Factory website (www.forexfactory.com/news.php) is a resource that I value much. please see Figure 22 for a screenshot of the section.

For example, if I were to take a decision on directional trade of a particular currency pair, I would like to know few things before making that decision such as is there any forthcoming news that might impact one or both the currencies in the pair, what's the sentiment in the market and how traders are viewing the currency pair's current and future direction etc. Although, this may not be immediately relevant for the type of trading discussed in this book, but as you learn more about this market, you would need these details for your trading decisions.

Sid Bhattacharjee

Figure 22: News section of the Forex Factory
Courtesy: Forexfactory.com, 2014

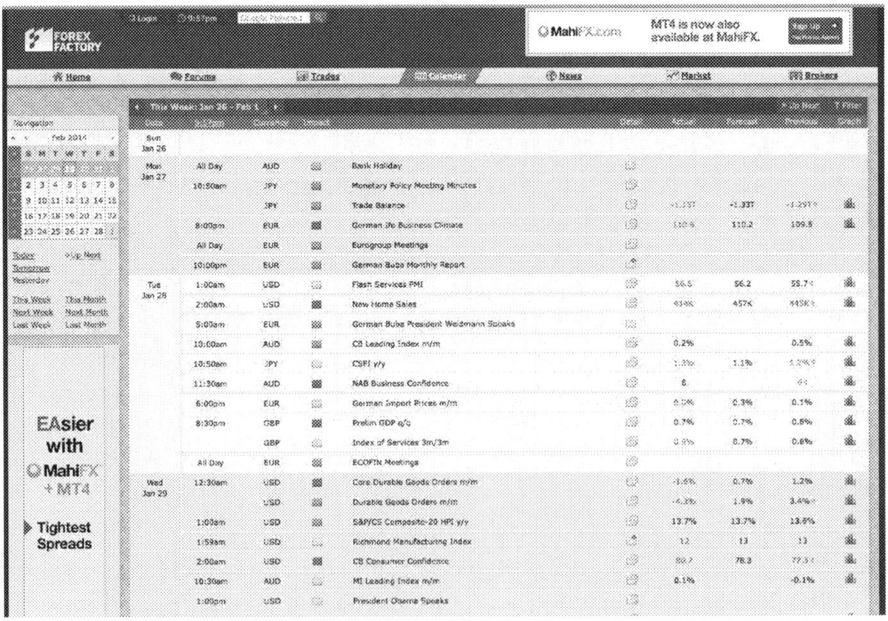

Figure 23: Economic calendar from Forex Factory
Courtesy: Forexfactory.com, 2014

Getting back to the discussion on economic calendar, I am providing the screenshot of the economic calendar from Forex Factory at Figure 23 to show you what it looks like and how to use the information provided in the calendar.

Please note that the calendar is set to Australian Eastern Standard Time (AEST) as I live in Australia and follow AEST for trading. You can set the calendar to your local time, matching it with your trading time. Just click on the time on the upper-right corner of the screen, then it will take you to a page where you can select your own time zone. Save it, and the calendar will be adjusted to your local time. It is very critical to get this right so you do not have to calculate when an economic report is coming out at your local time.

From Figure 23, it appears that there is a report coming from National Australia Bank (NAB) at 11:30AM on business confidence and that report will have high impact on Australian Dollar (AUD).

It is important that a trader stays away from trading any instrument such as forex involving AUD one hour before and after the release of the economic report under discussion. Why? Simply because of the high-impact nature of the report. Any asset involving AUD can move quite unpredictably in one direction or the other in a choppy manner, depending upon whether or not the economic report is favourable to the AUD currency. For trading binary options, we would like the currency pair to move in a steady direction, depending upon the chosen time frame, and not in a choppy manner as economic reports often confuses the market immediately on release. After the report is digested by the market and its effect understood, the market settles and either continues its original course or reverses its course.

Another of my favourite source of economic events and calendar is from very popular business news channel called Bloomberg. Bloomberg has its own business news television channel with Asian, European and American versions. You can subscribe to it if you want. It is also available for free on the Internet.

So the bottom line is that traders are best advised to stay away from trading relevant instruments when a report is due for release as per the economic calendar.

Tool No. 5: A Plan

You might have heard this quite-often-quoted saying: 'If you fail to prepare, you prepare to fail.' It's like if you are in warfare, you would need to have a plan of action as to how you attack your enemy. Please do not think for a moment that I mean the financial market is your enemy. It's not an enemy or a friend. It's the place where you go to do business and earn money. If it is of that importance, then surely you will need to have a plan. So what's the plan? Let's attempt to have a plan, a draft one to start with, and we might need to fine-tune that as we go along with our trading career.

The first principle of having a trading plan is that you would invest only as much money as you can afford to lose that wouldn't change your lifestyle. Let's say that amount is $5,000. You would have set aside the money somewhere (in a piggy bank or some bank account), hoping to do something that you hadn't yet planned for. I am suggesting this because this money is not your mainstream income or savings, and as such, in the unlikely event that this money becomes unavailable to you, it wouldn't jeopardize your finances. So we start our planning process with $5,000 in our trading account and build the plan from the ground up.

The second principle that I strongly urge you to follow is that in any given trade, you shouldn't be investing any more than 1% of your starting capital, preferably even smaller, maybe 0.5%. This means that in one trade, you are going to invest $50 or less. That's 1% of the initial starting capital. Let's say you want to be even more conservative and invest only 0.5% of the initial capital, which would be $25 per trade.

Unfortunately, some brokers have a requirement of a minimum investment per trade, and $25 may not be right for all brokers. For example, at the time of the writing of this book, IG Markets does not allow trading for less than $37 per trade, whereas with CLM, you could trade with as low as $1 per trade. I thought, in that respect, CLM is a great broker to start with as you can test your trading strategy with less than the cost of a Freddo chocolate! So for the moment, let's go with $50 per trade—unless you want to start with a higher starting capital, such as $7,400, where 0.5% would be $37, which is the minimum trading investment in Sprint Markets if you were trading with IG Markets. Brokers may change the minimum and maximum investment per trade to manage the risk at your end as well as at their end, so please do check with your broker at the time of placing trades.

Why such a small amount per trade? Simple answer is, we would like to put the odds in our favour by making as many number of trades as possible within the available time and also by making the successful trades to be at least 60% of the total trades. If you invest only a small amount per trade, it gives you more chances to take more trades and hence gives you higher chances of making more successful trades.

By the way, if you are wondering, what's the minimum successful percentage of trades needed just to break-even, then this is calculated as follows:

Minimum % successful trades = 100% / (100% + % profit per trade)

If your broker pays 80% return on successful trades then you would need a minimum of 55.6% successful trades to break-even. Similarly, with 75% return on investment, you would need a minimum of 57.1% successful trades to break-even. This is gives you an indication of what's the minimum percentage of successful trades you would need to keep your trading account intact as anything above those minimum figures, you will make profit.

The next step in our trading process is to start with an amount that you would like to earn in a day. Let's say you would like to earn $250 a day. This translates to about $5,500 a month, assuming 22 trading days in a month. I guess that's the average salary in Australia or in equivalent currencies in many other countries.

Let's go back to the table from which we had started the whole discussion on trading sprint options. It is reproduced here again but with modifications to reflect a few other scenarios and actual returns that your broker offers. The table is based on ten trades so that you get an idea of how many trades you would need to reach your goal of earning $250 a day.

So in summary, here are the inputs to Table 2:

Investment per trade: $50
Potential profit per trade: $40 or 80% of investment
Total return per trade: $90
Potential loss per trade: $50

Please note that in every winning trade, you will be returned the original invested amount and the profit. So when you win with $50 invested in a trade, you get back $90, which is made up of $50 and 80% profit on $50 or $40.

Table 2 Possible returns with various percentages of winning trades

Total Trades	Winners	Losers	Amount won	Amount lost	Net profit
10	0	10	$0	$500	-$500
10	1	9	$40	$450	-$410
10	2	8	$80	$400	-$320
10	3	7	$120	$350	-$230
10	4	6	$160	$300	-$140
10	5	5	$200	$250	-$50
10	6	4	$240	$200	$40
10	7	3	$280	$150	$130
10	8	2	$320	$100	$220
10	9	1	$360	$50	$310
10	10	0	$400	$0	$400

From the table above, the inference we can draw is that there are a number of combinations by which your daily goal could be achieved. You could have 70% success rate or 7 winners out of 10 trades but would need about 20 trades at the same success rate to make it to $260 a day. Or you could have just over 80% success rate or eight winners out of ten trades and come pretty close to your daily goal.

In Chapter 9, we are going to explore how many trades we are able to take typically in a day within the suggested trading hours and what the possible success rate is. That will give you an idea of how much money you will need to invest to get to your daily goal, but always make sure that you follow the two golden rules of investment:

1. You will invest only as much as you can afford to lose without changing your lifestyle.

2. You will invest no more than 1% of your trading capital per trade—
    better if it is 0.5%.

So now we have a plan that tells us that we need to make so many trades a day and that out of those trades, we will need so many trades to be winners for us to make the amount of money that we have aimed for.

— **End of Chapter 6** —

CHAPTER 7

Your Mind: The Most Important Tool Ever

Although this book is not intended to be a book on personal development or anything to do with motivation, I thought I will include a chapter on this nevertheless. During my journey through the trading career, as I kept learning various trading instruments in my quest to learn more, I became more spiritually aware and conscious of stuff around us that I never knew existed. In this chapter, I would like to give you some impression of that as I have a feeling that you might come across those at some point in time, and you might even rediscover yourself in the process—something that I have done myself over the years. I would sincerely request you to read this chapter before you start trading as you will need to be mentally prepared to do so. The sole purpose of this chapter is for you to uncover and discover some facts that you might have believed consciously or subconsciously and the effect they will have on the results. For example, if you have had negative thoughts about money, even if you have the best tools and resources, you will find a way to sabotage yourself and prevent yourself from making money.

Our thoughts guide our actions, and actions give you the result. If you think that money is hard to come by, then either you will think you will need to work very hard to get the money or you will think you don't want to work too hard because you are happy with your current situation and content with whatever money you have from work or business. Please remember, our brain is wired to guide us to make decisions that do not bring any harm to us or have little risk, so you will perhaps take the path of least resistance. I am summarizing some of the popular beliefs below, and you might be able to correlate with some or all of those, and unless you have cleared your mind of those negative thoughts about money, I suggest you do not start trading.

Let's look at what we think about money or what our money beliefs are one by one and check the reality of each one so that we are mentally more prepared for having a little more money.

Money Is the Root of All Evil

You might have heard over and over again that money is the root of all evils. Most of us have grown up with that being told to us by parents, families, friends, and people around us. Is that really so, that money is the root of all evils? Think about it again. Who are the people saying that? Perhaps the people who do not have much of money or at least not the wealthy ones. So what we do not have enough of, we call it root of evil! Just think of it once. Our society is so organized that you need money for everything around you—be it buying a bottle of water or sending your children to school or taking a short holiday or donating to your favourite charity, and almost everything around you. So when money is so much needed for everything that we want or desire, how could that be the root of all evil? I would rather say that the lack of money is the root of all evil.

Secondly, let's argue it in a different way; money is made of paper and metals, and these are materials of some kind with molecules, atoms, and nucleus. I do not think any sensible person will call atoms and molecules evil. Before money was invented, there was the barter system that our ancestors used. They used goats, sheep, and garden produce as currency in exchange for something else. Do you know if any sensible person will call goats, sheep, and vegetables evil? So if that's the case, why would notes and coins be evil? Money is not evil or root of evil. It is us who give meanings to things around us. It is simply not true that money is the root of all evil. It is the lack of money that's the root of all evil.

In Indian mythology, the goddess of wealth is Lakshmi; she is the daughter of the goddess Durga, the deity with ten hands created by the gods in heaven to rid Mother Earth of demons and evils. Lakshmi is worshipped by millions of Indians at their homes so that she can bring wealth to the family. I haven't read anything in the Indian mythology, which is thousands of years old, that says money is evil or having wealth is evil. I am still in the lookout for evidence of the origin of this myth!

Money Cannot Buy Happiness

I hear this all the time from various people—again, mostly from people who either always complain of not having enough money or have just enough to get around. An often-repeated quote tells me otherwise: 'People who say that money can't buy happiness just don't know where to shop.' And if I look around, I find more proof against the argument that money cannot buy happiness than for it.

When you are able to do something that you are passionate about, wouldn't that make you happy? When you are able to spend more time with your family and work less, wouldn't that make you happy? If you are able to donate to a charity that changes the lives of people, wouldn't that make you happy? If you are able to bring smiles on the faces of your children by taking them to a surprise holiday, wouldn't that make you happy?

Some people would argue that money cannot bring health. I feel that's also a myth. Money will let you have the best treatment possible and keep you healthy. I would say that if you have enough money and you are happy being busy in doing things that you are passionate about, you will live a fuller life and will be healthy as you will not nurture negative thoughts in your mind about the lack of money.

I hope you now understand where I am going with this myth. It is simply not true that money cannot buy happiness. It is what we have been led to believe by people around us who do not have enough money. So dispel any notion in your mind that money cannot bring happiness.

You Must Work Hard for Money

This is another myth that people have believed for ages. This perhaps come from the early time when human beings were evolving and they had to do everything physically, such as building their own home and growing fruits and vegetables to feed themselves and their family. In the modern age, you can get a lot of things done without even having to lift your finger as you have resources at your disposal to do all the things that wouldn't have been possible in the past.

At the writing of this book, *Forbes* just announced Bill Gates, founder of Microsoft, as the world's richest man. Bloomberg reported that he had made $11.5 billion last year. A few other people who had made more than $10 billion in 2013 were Mark Zuckerberg (Facebook), Warren Buffet (Berkshire Hathaway), Jeff Bezos (Amazon), and Sergey Brin (Google). How much hard work do you think these people have done to earn that big money?

You might argue that these people already had tens of billions of dollars so it was easy for them to make $10 billion. I think you will agree that these people have wisely invested in one or more very profitable companies where they knew that the value of the shares will go higher for a variety of reasons: either the management team of the company is good to deliver better results or there is an increased demand for the products and services of those companies or the company has entered into a new alliance to have increased sales or the company has released a new product that is going to be in great demand in the coming years, and so on and so forth. The key here is that all these super wealthy people have learnt where to invest and how much to invest, and they know the possible outcomes beforehand and are prepared for an alternative action. No hard work was involved whatsoever.

To put your mind at ease, let me give you an example from an ordinary man's perspective. If you had known in 2001 that China is going to go through rapid industrialization and would need iron and steel to support the growth, you would have considered buying the shares of companies which produces iron ores. One such company is BHP Billiton Ltd (BHP) in Australia, which produces the lion's share of iron ore production in the world. If you had bought 2,500 shares of BHP in February 2001 at $4 a share, it would have cost you $10,000. In the middle of 2007, the BHP shares had hit over $44, so your $10,000 investment would have turned into $110,000. In other words, your investment of $10,000 would be grown 11 times in a short span of 6 years. What hard work would you have needed to do to get this astronomical return on investment? Nothing, absolutely nothing. So please dispel any myth that you need to do hard work to make money. It is not true. You need to educate yourself and invest wisely to make money. Hard work is an inefficient way of making money.

I just gave only a few examples. You might have other money beliefs or myths that you thought were true. Lies repeated many times tend to sound like truth. So be among people who have a healthy view of life and money and not with the ones who curse wealth.

Trading is in the mind, meaning all it takes for you to be a successful trader is a mind that's comfortable to deal with the perseverance, tension, anxiety, and all such strong emotions in a disciplined manner. I will deal with all these in detail in this chapter as it's the strongest tool you possess to be a successful trader. I am not a psychologist and I am not attempting to be one for the purpose of this kind of trading. But please do realize that despite all the tools you are in possession of, you might be overwhelmed by emotions as it involves money and money often evokes strong emotions of greed and fear.

If you are not one of those, then you are a small minority, and you perhaps already possess the great skill to be successful. However, as your trading account grows and you start dealing with large sums of money in a trade, you might suddenly feel the emotions of greed and fear, which you did not feel when dealing with smaller amounts. I am saying this because each one among us has something like a thermostat within us, which decides our comfort level for dealing with various emotions at various levels.

Please always have a purpose for money. Money itself is just a few pieces of paper incapable of doing anything. We need to give money a purpose. Money gives you options. This purpose of money is what should drive an individual and not the money itself. You might have plenty of money in the bank but still live a miserable life. Start thinking about what you would do if you have a secondary source of money. What would you do with that? Connect that with some emotional outcome, and you will rediscover that money is a great source of so many positive outcomes that you wouldn't have thought of in the past.

As an example, if I wanted a secondary source of income, I could work part-time. If I could work part-time, I could spend more time playing a sport or a musical instrument that I have long waited to learn but never could find time or money to afford. Or you might say I could spend little more time with my child, who is growing so fast. Or you might say that I would like to travel around the world, a passion I've always had. I hope you get the idea.

There are two things that you should always connect to money. One is the deeply emotional outcome arising out of your own personal need or the needs of your near and dear ones, and the other is that your money should serve a beneficial purpose to the people around you or someone whose need is bigger than your own. You could sponsor a child, for example. And the more you give, the more you will get. That's the law of nature. Money should circulate. That's the best use of money. To give an example, if money circulates, the country is economically healthy as everybody gets and moves the money around. On the contrary, if governments and businesses hoard money or stop spending, the economy would be unhealthy as there would be unemployment, workers would not have jobs, and so on.

Famous Irish author Oscar Wilde had made an interesting comment which I would like to reproduce here so you would know that going after money is not a bad thing after all! He once said that 'anyone who lives within their means suffers from a lack of imagination'. I think the meaning is quite profound, and I hope you will agree.

Managing Emotions in Wins and Losses

Money tends to evoke strong emotional responses for various reasons as mentioned above, and we often can't handle losses very well. I have seen and known many people who had a good start with business or trading, and after one loss or a couple of losses, they gave it up completely, never to return in that business and trading career.

Losses are part of the game. Even the best sports team in the world also loses games here and there. But why are they the best team? It is because they are consistent in their efforts, and consistent effort brings consistent results. Even individuals might have had a very poor success in all previous endeavours but eventually come out with great success. Abraham Lincoln is said to be a nobody from nowhere. He had failed in business, failed in family life, but went on to become one of the most memorable personalities of the modern world. So if you have a string of losses, think that this is part of the game plan, and move on.

As mentioned earlier, our brain is wired to protect us from losses of any kind—physical, mental, or emotional. This is not the fault of any of us. This is how the primitive human evolved, but unfortunately, a part of the brain has remained primitive and has not evolved with modern times. So we are generally risk-averse, always try to take the path of least resistance, and avoid confrontations as we anticipate harm to ourselves, and our brains generate hormones to fight or flee.

We will need to reorient our brains to handle such situations so that we take little more rational decisions and handle apparently poor-looking situations and turn them into something positive and in line with our hopes and aspirations. Let's attempt to get over this with an example.

We all have been toddlers at some point in our lives although we may not recollect our childhood in so much detail as adults. When we first wanted to stand up, we might have fallen back on the floor a few times. Or when we realized that it was hard to stand up on our own, we might have grabbed on a stool or the bedside or a table to stand up. Once we successfully stood up, we wanted to take our first step. Again, we might have fallen a few times and might have injured ourselves in the process. Did we stop walking after that? We didn't as I know most healthy adults do walk.

Should that be different from the situation in trading? Not at all. If you have had a few losses, you shouldn't be deterred from your goal of making a living from trading as it is no different from the toddler falling a few times before learning to walk but learning to walk nevertheless. The only reason many of us stop doing what we had ventured to do is the fear of further losses arising out of our learning from experiences and from the environment.

Another simple example will illustrate this better. If you are born in a family of abalone divers where you have seen since birth that your parents and family members are diving into the ocean, fighting sharks, and bringing tons of abalones on the surface, would you be scared to jump into the ocean? Perhaps not. On the contrary, if you are born into a family of office-going people and have been brought up watching your parents and family members going to the office every day, would you be scared to jump into the ocean in your next holiday? Most likely, yes especially when you hear about the sharks. It is our mental conditioning as we have grown in our life from childhood to adolescence to adulthood. Some of these conditioning are genetically coded, and some are caused by our environment. But the very good news is that these conditioning can be changed at any time in life, and there are various methods of doing it.

So when you have a string of losses in a trade, think that you are going through the training period and that it is OK to falter a few times but eventually you will stand up and run.

If you are emotionally so attached to your big picture in life, that itself will change your conditioning to a very great extent. You will learn to handle minor losses here and there as these are similar to the toddler falling and injuring himself before he learns to walk.

So let me simplify the few important points in this chapter:

1. Do not try to fight the negative thoughts you have about money. Just believe that money is a good thing to have for the reasons explained.
2. Connect money with an emotional outcome as explained in this chapter.
3. Look at the bigger picture of your personal goals, and start your journey with confidence, belief, and faith.

— **End of Chapter 7** —

CHAPTER 8

Putting All These Together:
Preparing the Desktop

OK, let's summarize what we have learnt so far and what tools we have in our hands to put our very first trade through.

We have learnt what instrument we are trading, viz. binary options or digital options, which is also called sprint options if you are with IG Markets. We have also learnt which broker we are going to use for the purpose. You have a choice; three are mentioned in this book for the platforms they offer, viz. IG Markets, Stockpair, or CLM. And lastly, we have learnt what chart we will be using and what time frame the chart will be set to. So here is the list of things that we would need before we are able to initiate a trade:

1. a computer with fast and reliable Internet connection, preferably cable or ADSL2+
2. a subscription to a broker, IG Markets or Stockpair or CLM Forex for reasons mentioned before
3. a quality Web browser, such as Google Chrome if using Windows computer or Apple's own Safari browser if using Apple Mac, for trading with IG Markets and Stockpair (you do not need a browser for trading with CLM Forex)
4. a quality timer (you will soon understand the importance of it).

While the first three items above are obvious requirements, I would lay no less importance to a quality 5- or 15-minute timer, depending upon the time frame you choose to trade with. In all the succeeding examples, we will be trading off a five-minute candlestick chart, in which case you will need to look at the chart every five minutes for the decision to enter a trade. I have also discussed an alternative timeframe trading later in Chapter 10 where you would need a 15 minute timer instead of 5 minute timer. It becomes very difficult to continue to keep looking at the computer screen for a prolonged period—at least that's what I found it to be. So I wanted to find a way to look at the screen only when I am required to in order to make my life a little easier or to keep doing something else I like, such as reading a book.

The screenshot below at Figure 24 is that of a 5-minute timer for iPhone. Similar timers are also available for a 15-minute interval and other intervals. It was available for download free of charge from iTunes store till few months ago, but recently a small amount is being charged for all timers from the same developer. As an option, you could also use a computer based timer, mostly available for free from Internet. Just do a google search for a timer and you might find one that is good for the purpose.

Figure 24: A sample of the free five-minute timer for iPhone.

I set the 5-minute timer in such a way that the timer goes off about 40 seconds before the start of the 5-minute candle in the candlestick chart. Candlestick charts are synced with the clock of your computer, which in turn would perhaps be synced with the Internet clock or any other reliable time source. So when the timer is properly set up, I get a beep, say at 7.39.20. That's 40 seconds before the next candle at 7.40. These 40 seconds gives me just enough time to have a quick glance at the charts and see if a trade is possible and if any parameters need to be set in the trading platform.

We are almost there with our tools and resources, but there are three more things we need to know about before we click our first trade. These are the following: What forex pair are we trading? Which time of the day is best suited to trade? And most importantly, what conditions must be met before we take our first trade? The last part is described in detail in Chapter 9, where we look for set-ups to enter into a trade. But for now, let's focus on the first two points.

Which forex pair do we trade?

The two common terms used to define the price movement of an asset are *rangebound* and *trending*. *Rangebound* means that the price movements of the asset are by and large within a predefined range of high and low values or between a support line and resistance line. Refer to Chapter 6 for a refresher if you need to. *Trending*, on the other hand, means that the price movement is directional or the price is generally moving in one direction, either upwards or downwards.

The prices are rangebound when there is not much activity in the market or when there is no economic event that influences one of the currencies in the pair. On the contrary, if there is an economic event or even a political event that can have an effect on the economy of the countries to which the currencies belong, the price can start trending. Trending can be short term or long term as can be seen by the time frame of the chart. Sometimes the short-term trend may be opposite of the long-term trend, but in the example shown in Figure 25 and Figure 26, the short-term trend is in the same direction as in the long-term trend for the popular currency pair AUDUSD.

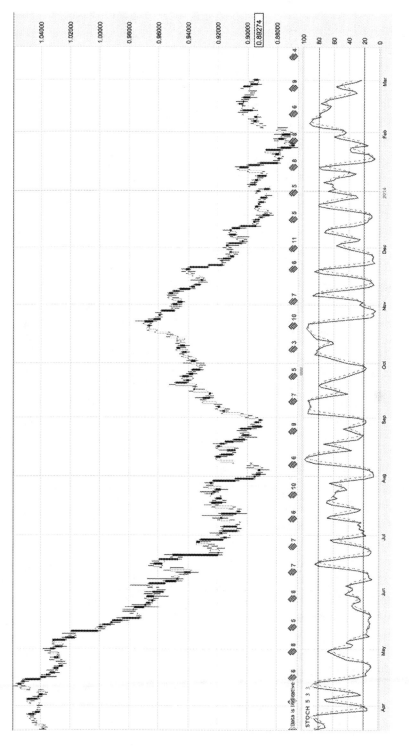

Figure 25: AUDUSD daily chart showing downtrend.

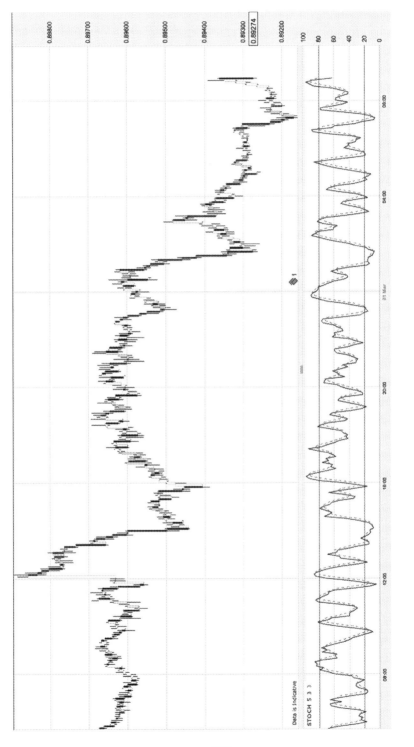

Figure 26: AUDUSD five-minute chart also showing short-term downtrend.

The two criteria that we are looking for in a currency pair for us to trade binary options are liquidity and that the currency pair is rangebound.

As mentioned in Chapter 2, EURUSD is the most traded currency pair in the forex market. Since this is the most traded currency pair across institutional investors—importer and exporter and speculators alike—there is enough liquidity in the currency pair to ensure that there are enough movements in the price. Also, the two currencies making up the pair represent two very large economies of the world. As such, the price movements are quite controlled most of the time except after a major economic event. Refer to Chapter 6 for a refresher. So EURUSD seems to fit our requirement quite nicely.

Being rangebound is a feature of a currency pair and also of the time of the day. While we found EURUSD to be a currency pair with liquidity, let's see if it is also rangebound—at least, for some time of the day. If you look at the time when the US equity market is closed—that is, 8 a.m. AEST to about 3 p.m. AEST—most of the currency pairs seem to range, particularly the ones which has the currency of the country where the equity market is closed. For example, if there are no major economic news or events, currency pairs involving currencies from Australia (AUD), Japan (JPY), and New Zealand (NZD) might trend during this time of the day, whereas currency pairs involving currencies of countries such as Europe (EUR), Switzerland (CHF), and USA (USD) might generally be rangebound. Since businesses and commercial institutions in those countries are open, it is likely that currency exchange will take place in large volumes, affecting the movement, and hence, the currency pair might assume a directional movement and trend. Figure 27 shows the EURUSD currency pair ranging between two reasonably well-defined price levels for almost more than half of the trading day. This is great for trading binary options as we know that the movements are fairly predictable during these hours of the day, and that's what we want.

One of the most important factors affecting the movement of the currency pairs is the interest rates set by the central banks of the countries to which those currencies belong. For example, if the Reserve Bank of Australia (RBA, the central bank of Australia) decides to increase the interest rate to rein in the inflation, this will result in almost all currency pairs involving AUD—such as AUDUSD, AUDJPY, and AUDNZD—to trend upwards and for EURAUD and GBPAUD to trend downwards. Since the global financial crisis, the central banks of most of the developed economies have set the interest rates to historical low (e.g. Japan and USA have interest rates close to zero). As the economic environment improves and inflation creeps up, one would expect that the central banks of those countries will increase the interest rates, and this will result in the currency pairs involving the currencies of those countries to trend to a new level where it might settle after a while.

But for now, let's focus on EURUSD as our currency of choice, and also we have found what time during the day we should be trading binary options.

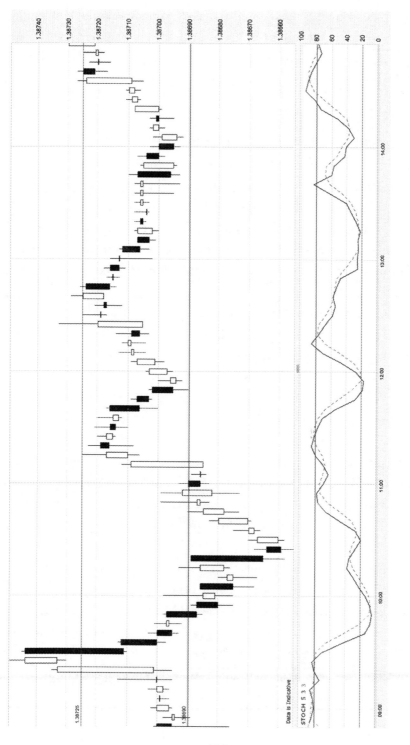

Figure 27: EURUSD five-minute chart from 9 a.m. to 3 p.m. AEST

Now that we have got all the tools we need to trade, let's do some trading. But before we do so, we need to set up our tools in the computer, starting with the charting platform followed by the trading platform. Once these are ready, we will look for a set-up to take our trades.

Preparing the Charting Window

Trading binary options or any other instrument in a financial market involves making decisions based on the historical value of an asset and market sentiment, assessed either through fundamental or technical analysis. For trading binary options, we will need to have the chart of the asset readily visible for us to make a quick technical analysis and place a trade. In this section, I am going to discuss the charting window set-up for the three broker platforms mentioned.

We are going to have two windows in your browser to start trading. The first one is the chart window, and overlapping the chart window is the trading platform window. This only applies, however, to IG Markets and Stockpair but not to Core Liquidity Markets for reasons explained later in this chapter.

Why two windows and why overlapping? The simple reason is that our trading decisions are going to be based on the price action in the chart window, and once you decide to place the trade, you will need the trading platform to place that trade. If the windows were not overlapping, it would take a few valuable seconds to switch between the chart window and trading platform window, and that could sometimes prove detrimental to your profitability as price might have already moved from the price at which you would have wanted to enter the trade.

This particularly is important when you are using a five-minute chart for trading. After all, a few seconds is a long time when all you have got is five minutes. By the way, do not panic on this five-minute-trading thing as I am going to give an alternative trading strategy where you will have more time to place a trade and where, most likely, a few seconds will not matter much. So hang in there. The alternative trading strategy is not superior or inferior to the five-minute trading. It's a matter of preference, and as you start trading, you will soon discover the best strategy that suits you. I personally like the five-minute chart for trading binary options.

Irrespective of whatever time frame you use for trading, 5 minutes or 15 minutes, it is always a good idea to have both the trading platform and charting platform visible to you at the same time. Overlapping the charting platform and trading platform is a good idea for laptop computers or desktops with one display. But if you have access to two monitors, you could have the charting platform on one display and the trading platform on the other. I personally use and like this set-up, but this is in no way a requirement for trading.

Setting Up Charting for IG Markets

Fire up the computer and log in to your account. Just type the login name and password that you have registered at the time of opening the account. There are various sections in the screen that you would like to be aware of as you start setting up the charting platform. All of those are marked.

The home screen has a few sections that you need to be familiar with. The educational video on the IG Markets' website will provide a lot of information as mentioned in Chapter 6, but for now, let's look at the ones that we need to prepare to start trading.

The first among those is the watch list. I suggest you create a watch list of forex pairs that you might use for your trading. Once set up, it will help you quickly open a chart. You can create a watch list by clicking on New Watchlist on the lower-left corner of the screen. You might name that as Forex Major as an example. You could name it anything you like! On my trading platform, it is named as My Watchlist, and this comes with the platform itself. Once you have created a new watch list or have used the My Watchlist, you can fill it in with any trading asset type you like.

I suggest for now that you just fill it in only with the forex pair that you will be trading. To put the first forex pair in the watch list, type EURUSD in the search box at the upper-left corner of the home screen. It will come up with a few options, choose Spot FX EUR/USD and click on the button. This opens up a new window and several other versions of the same asset, EURUSD. Click on the arrow for the drop downmenu next to the button for Spot FX

EURUSD. It will give you a few options, such as deal ticket, order to open, insight, and chart. Choose the option for Add to Watchlist on that screen. This process may be repeated for any other forex pair or any other instrument that you might like to add to your watch list.

Once the watch list is ready with the list of forex pairs, we are ready to open the chart of the favourite forex pair that we will be trading. Let's say that your chosen forex pair is EURUSD which you will be trading as discussed before. Once you open the chart, try to click on the button first to detach the chart from the trading platform. Once the chart is detached, go full screen by clicking on the appropriate button on the upper-right corner of the chart window. The chart, when it is opened for the first time on your trading platform, looks like the one in Figure 28. This is the bare-bone chart that we need to dress up before we can start being able to read it properly.

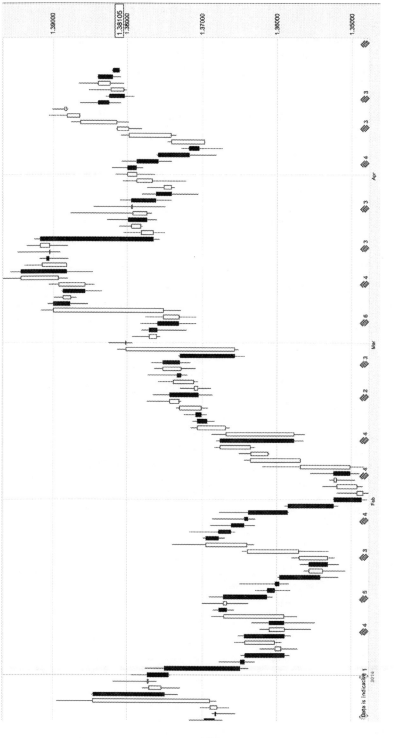

Figure 28: The EURUSD chart as it is opened for the first time.

137

The first thing to do is to set the chart to the time frame that is suitable for our type of trading. Our initial chart setting is going to be a five-minute time frame. The reason is described in the following chapter. You can do that by clicking on the Daily button on the upper-left corner of the screen. This will give you various options for setting the chart. Pick the 5m. So the new five-minute chart is going to look something like the one on Figure 29. Close the time options by clicking the X button on the upper-right corner of the chart.

We now have the five-minute chart that we are going to use for trading. The next thing to do is to draw the support and resistance lines in the chart. For this, you will need to click on the Drawings button. This will give you a few options. Click on the horizontal line. This will give you the option to place a horizontal line anywhere in the chart. Let's first check where the prices have bounced over the visible section of the chart. With the help of the horizontal line option, let's place lines at locations as shown in Figure 30. If you happen to place a line in the wrong place, you can always drag the line to another location. For this, you need not go to the drawing menu.

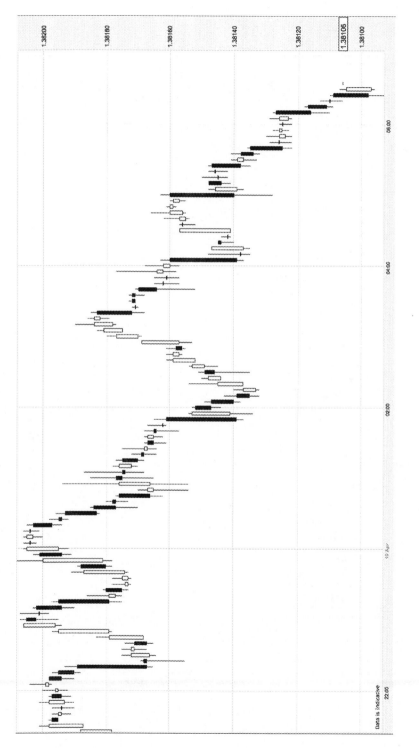

Figure 29: The five-minute EURUSD chart.

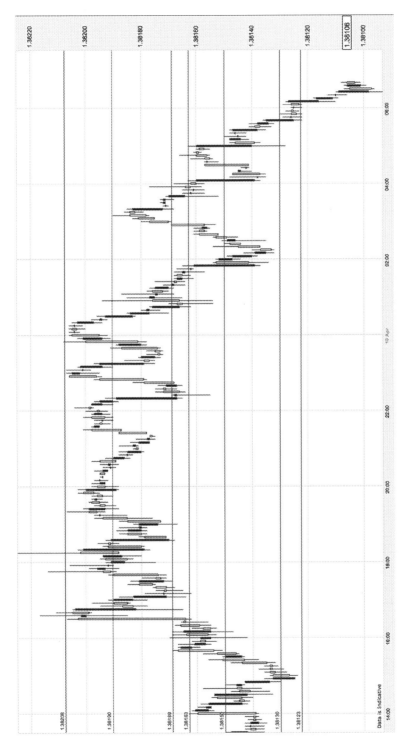

Figure 30: Support and resistance lines on the chart.

We now have a chart set with the right time frame and with the support and resistance lines drawn on it. The next piece of technical analysis tool we need on the chart is the slow stochastic indicator. IG Markets' platform offers a range of technical analysis tools accessible from the chart by clicking the text TECHNICAL ANALYSIS on the upper-left corner of the chart. On clicking this, you will have access to a range of tools, including stochastic indicator marked as 'STOCH'. Click on that, and you will immediately notice the indicator at the bottom of the chart. While the stochastic indicator has three setting options for parameters as described in Chapter 6, I would recommend you leave the values at default, which are at 5, 3, 3 for %K period, slow period, and %D periods, respectively.

This completes our charting set-up for the IG Markets' platform. Your chart set-up should look very similar to the one shown in Figure 31.

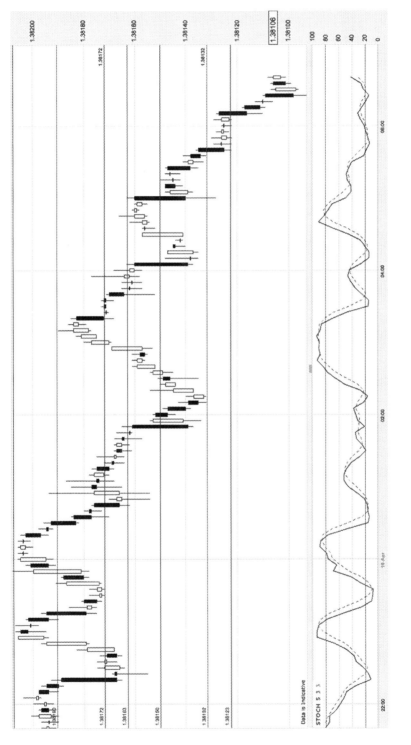

Figure 31: The five-minute EURUSD chart with all the technical analyses.

142

Setting Up Charting for Stockpair

If you decide not to use IG Markets for your broker or are unable to sign up with IG Markets for some reason, then you have the option to choose Stockpair or CLM Forex. Let's discuss Stockpair and see what we need to do for trading on that platform. Please note that most of the new-generation brokers of binary options who provide Web-based trading of binary options, including Stockpair, do not provide a full-featured charting facility. It provides a basic one only, which is almost of no use for the purpose of trading. So you will need to get separate charting software from another source.

My suggested charting software is MetaTrader 4, or MT4, available for free from MetaQuotes (http://www.metatrader4.com/traders). Actually, MT4 is a full-featured trading platform also offered by a range of brokers, but since you are going to use only the charting feature of MT4, please visit the URL mentioned above and download the MT4 software package to your computer. As you might have just noticed, contrary to IG Markets, where you do not need to install any software to run the charting and trading platform, trading with any other brokers of binary options might need charting software to be installed on your computer. Installation of MT4 is very straightforward. After you have downloaded the software, please go through the instruction on the URL mentioned above if you are unfamiliar with it.

Please note a few things. First, MT4 runs only on a Windows PC. If you intend to trade on an Apple Mac computer, then there may be additional software needed for running the MT4 platform in a Mac OS environment. Most of the average computer users may not be so conversant with running a Windows application in a Mac OS environment, so my suggestion for you is to use a Windows PC if you are going to use the MT4 charting platform. The second point to note is, the EURUSD or any other currency prices shown on the MT4 platform may or may not match with the prices shown on the broker platform, such as Stockpair. This is simply because the price feed are treated by brokers differently in terms of spread, and hence, the price presented to the end user varies with the broker.

Once you have installed the MT4 platform software on your Windows PC, you will need to sign up for a demo account with one of the broker options presented by the MT4 charting platform. Again, it is very straightforward.

You need to choose the broker to source the data feed for the platform, and MT4 will automatically set you up for the purpose. Please note that the broker of choice is given only for the data feed. It has no other implication, and you don't have to sign up with the broker in any form unless you decide to do that for some other reason, such as trading some other instrument with the broker.

Once the MT4 charting platform is installed on your computer, a data feed is available. You will need to set up the chart for you to be able to use it in a manner that helps you read the charts better. The default charting set-up in MT4 consists of four windows of four currency pairs arranged on the desktop in tile formation. You will need to maximize the EURUSD chart window so that you will see only one chart at a time.

Once you have done that, you will need to take the following actions to set up the chart properly:

1. From among the various charting options, you will need to choose Candlestick. This is available from the menu on the top. Select Candlestick.

2. The default candlestick colours on MT4 are hollow for *bull* (increasing) candlestick and green for *bear* (decreasing) candlestick. If you are comfortable with this colour scheme, leave it as it is. Alternatively, you might like to change the colours to something more readable, such as *green* for *bull* candlestick and *red* for *bear* candlestick. You can do that by going to the options and selecting the colours mentioned above.

3. For better readability, you might like to also change the colour of the background as the default background is black. You can leave it as it is if you so prefer, but if you want a white background like that of IG Markets' charting platform, then right-click on the chart and change the colour to white or some shade of white that's more soothing for your eyes.

4. Chart time frame will need to be changed to five minutes if it hasn't been yet. You can do that by selecting from the menu on the top.

5. You will need to draw *support* and *resistance* lines similar to how you may have read about doing the same on IG Markets' charting platform.

6. The last thing to do on MT4's charting platform is to include the stochastic indicator on the chart. You can do so by going to the navigation menu on the left. Expand it and locate the stochastic indicator. Once you drag on the indicator from the menu to the chart, it will ask for a few options. Select 5, 3, 3 on the options presented, and click Close to set up the stochastic indicator on your chart.

With the chart set-up done the way you want or as suggested, you do not repeat doing the same for other assets, such as USDJPY. You can save the template and apply it to any other charts. To do so, right-click on the chart, and select the appropriate button to save the template with a name of your choice. One suitable name would be, for example, Daily Income Binary Options. Once you have saved the template, you are ready to use the same set-up for the other charts. To do so, open the USDJPY chart, another asset that you may be trading. Right-click on the chart and select Daily Income Binary Options from the menu presented. With that, the USDJPY chart will be very similar to the EURUSD chart in terms of look and feel only.

That concludes setting up the MT4 chart on your computer. Presumption has been made that you are reasonably computer-literate and are able to do basic installation of software on your computer. If you are unfamiliar with any of the instructions in this subsection, please seek help from someone who can help you install the software and set up the chart as described. Alternatively, please visit the MT4 download URL mentioned above, and surf through the various help and FAQ sections to get the details of how to install and customize the charting platform to fit your requirements.

Setting Up Core Liquidity Markets' Charting Platform

As mentioned before, CLM uses the MT4 platform for trading. So setting up the charting platform is exactly similar to the one described for the MT4 platform for use for trading with Stockpair except that you will need to open the platform via the FX Lite icon. FX Lite is the additional piece of software you will need to install to trade binary options on CLM's MT4 platform. The installation instruction for MT4 and FX Lite is sent to you when you sign up with the broker. Installation is very easy and basically just a few clicks' work during the process. Once you open it, set up the charting application as described for MT4 for use with Stockpair.

The additional action required is that on the Market Watch window on the left, please right-click with your mouse to access the available menu options. In that, select Show All. This will bring up all the assets available to trade on the platform, which includes standard forex and binary options on forex, indices, and gold and silver. All symbols that are available to trade as binary options end with *bo*. For example, EURUSD binary option will show on the Market Watch window as *EURUSDbo* and so on. Since these are binary-options-related assets, please use these symbols for your charts. If you use only EURUSD on your chart and you'd like to trade binary options, then the platform will enter the trade as a regular forex trade, and the menu related to binary options wouldn't appear. Please note, this is the difference between trading binary options on MT4 and using MT4 as a charting tool for trading on another platform.

Preparing the Trading Platform Window

Once we are satisfied with the chart window and that all are set to go, next is to make sure that the trading platform is also ready for us to take the trade. In this section, we will discuss each of the trading platforms in detail for you to set up the trading platform before you place a trade.

Setting Up the IG Markets' Trading Platform

While the chart window is ready, switch to the main trading platform window or the Home window as you would do for any other application in Windows. Look at the upper-right corner of the IG Markets' Home window for the button Sprint Markets. On clicking this button, it will bring up a pop-up window with the heading 'Sprint Markets'. This is the window from which you will be trading.

This is the main trading window where we will record all actions for each and every trade. We need to dress up the window to make the desktop ready for trading. There are four settings that we will need to change for this purpose. Let's go one by one.

The first thing to make a change to is Market. We are going to click on the upper-right corner of the sister window, where you see AUD/USD. Choose EUR/USD from the list of options offered against the market as EURUSD is our chosen asset for trading as discussed in Chapter 2.

The second item to change in the window is to input the investment amount marked as Premium (AUD) immediately underneath Market. As discussed in Chapter 6, our investment per trade is going to be $50 as per our example, and we are going to type this amount in this box. If you start with a different trading account size, then you may type in your investment-per-trade figure here, which is based on 1% of your account size.

The third item to set up is Expiry. It is the time by which the trade will expire or, in simple terms, the time by which the value of your instrument must be *above* or *below* for you to win the trade. We are going to choose a 20-minute expiry, and we are going to do this by clicking on the clock right under the Premium button. You have the option to choose other expiry time as well as explained in an alternative strategy in Chapter 10. But for now, let's choose the 20-minute expiry from the options offered by clicking on the clock on the right of the Expiry button. On clicking the clock, you will be offered expiry options of 1 minute, 2 minutes, 5 minutes, 20 minutes, and 60 minutes. Choose 20 minutes, and leave it at that for now.

The only two other items we will need be aware of are Direction and Return, but only at the time when we are just about to enter into a trade. As the name implies, Direction gives you the option to choose the direction to which the market will go to on expiry of the option. The two options are Above and Below. If the market ends up being above the price at which you entered the trade on expiry, you will be paid the amount mentioned in the green box on the right of the Return button. The green box on the right of the Return button is also the button you will click to enter into a trade.

IG Markets offer 81% return on forex pairs and 75% return on most equity indices. So when you had chosen EURUSD in the Market option and typed in $50 in the Premium (AUD), the green box on the right of the Return button would show a return of $90.50, which is made up of $50 premium and profit of $40.50, which is 81% of premium $50. One good thing about IG Markets is that if the price on expiry is exactly the same as that when you had initiated the trade, you will receive a return of half of the investment or, in this case, $25. So for you to win a trade, EURUSD should be at least 0.00001 (the smallest fractional movement of the price) above the price at which you entered the trade.

So for now, let us leave the item Direction untouched and not click on the Submit button till we intend to enter into a trade.

Once we are done with setting up the items as mentioned above, we are almost ready to take the next step. There is one more thing to do; we need to be able to see the trading platform and the EURUSD chart at the same time. My preferred option is to have a bigger chart window overlapped by a reduced-sized trading platform. You might position the two windows in a manner that's more comfortable for you, but I like it that way simply because with about two-third of the screen occupied by the chart and one-thirds by the trading platform, it allows me to see the Open Positions window on the trading platform. When you are in a trade, you would like to see how your trade is performing, and that is available for you to see in the Open Positions window on the trading platform. But it is up to you how you want to make your desktop look like and convenient for you to trade.

When you are in a trade and you are 'in the money', meaning the price has moved in your chosen direction, the Open Positions window will show price movement in relation to the opening price, and the window colour will be blue. If your trade is 'out of money', or when the price has moved against your chosen direction, the window will be red in colour. So there is a visual indication of the status of the trade. I thought it was a good feature.

Setting Up Stockpair's Trading Platform

The basic set-up of Stockpair's trading platform is very similar to that of the IG Markets except that the names of the parameters are changed. So we will go through each of these parameters and preset them so that you can be ready to trade.

Once you log in to the Stockpair website, it will open up the trading platform, where you will need to input the parameters of interest, and these are the same as any other platform except that they are named differently. To start with, we will need to select the asset from the left side of the platform. In this case, we are going to select Currencies and then select EURUSD. The next parameter to select is the option Expiry Time. Please note that Stockpair offers a long range of expiry time, from 1 minute to 150 days. We are going to select "In the next 15 minutes" from the pull down menu, where it says, 'Will EUR/USD go up or down?' Please note that the broker does not offer 20 minute expiry, so we are selecting 15 minute. The next to select is the direction of movement of the asset, *up* or *down*. These are marked as arrows on two sides of the asset name EURUSD. Depending on your assessment, you may select either the *up* or *down* option.

The last but not the least to input to the platform is the amount of investment, which can be done on the right-hand side of the platform in the box Set Your Trade. In that box, in the amount row, you can type in an amount or pick one of the amounts listed in the pull-down menu. The only button you can click on to enter a trade is the big BUY button at the bottom of the box. But we are going to wait and do our analysis before we take the trade by clicking the BUY button.

Setting Up the Core Liquidity Market's Trading Platform

One of the good things about the CLM trading platform is that there is no separate charting and trading platform; both are in one combined screen. I thought this is a great advantage.

Please refer to Figure 32 for a screenshot of the CLM Forex trading platform.

Once you have ensured that the charting set-up is done as explained in the previous section, you are ready to trade except that usual set-ups, such as expiry time and investment, are required. For placing a trade, you will need to double-click the asset on the Market Watch window; it will open up a window where you will need to put the trading parameters. One issue I noticed is that once a trade is placed, the platform does not remember any of the previous settings. This means that you will have to set these parameters again for the next trade. Some may consider this an advantage so that you are ensuring that you are correctly setting the parameters rather than relying on the previous setting, which may not be right!

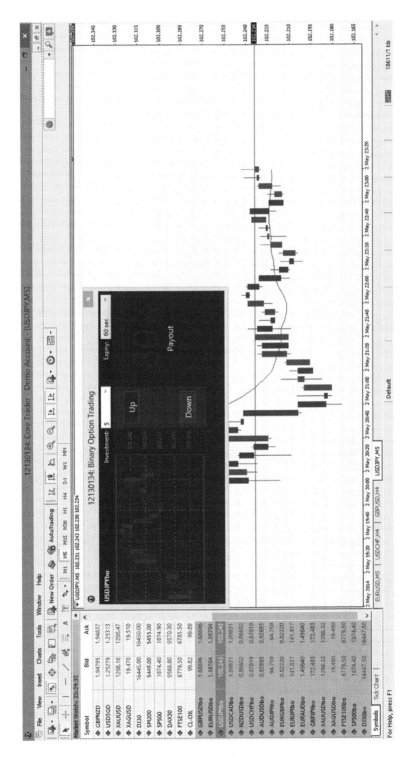

Figure 32: CLM Forex binary options trading platform.

150

I have also included a screenshot of the CLM Forex binary trading platform at Figure 33. The figure shows you how it looks like when a trade is in progress with associated details such as amount invested, expiry time and time remaining.

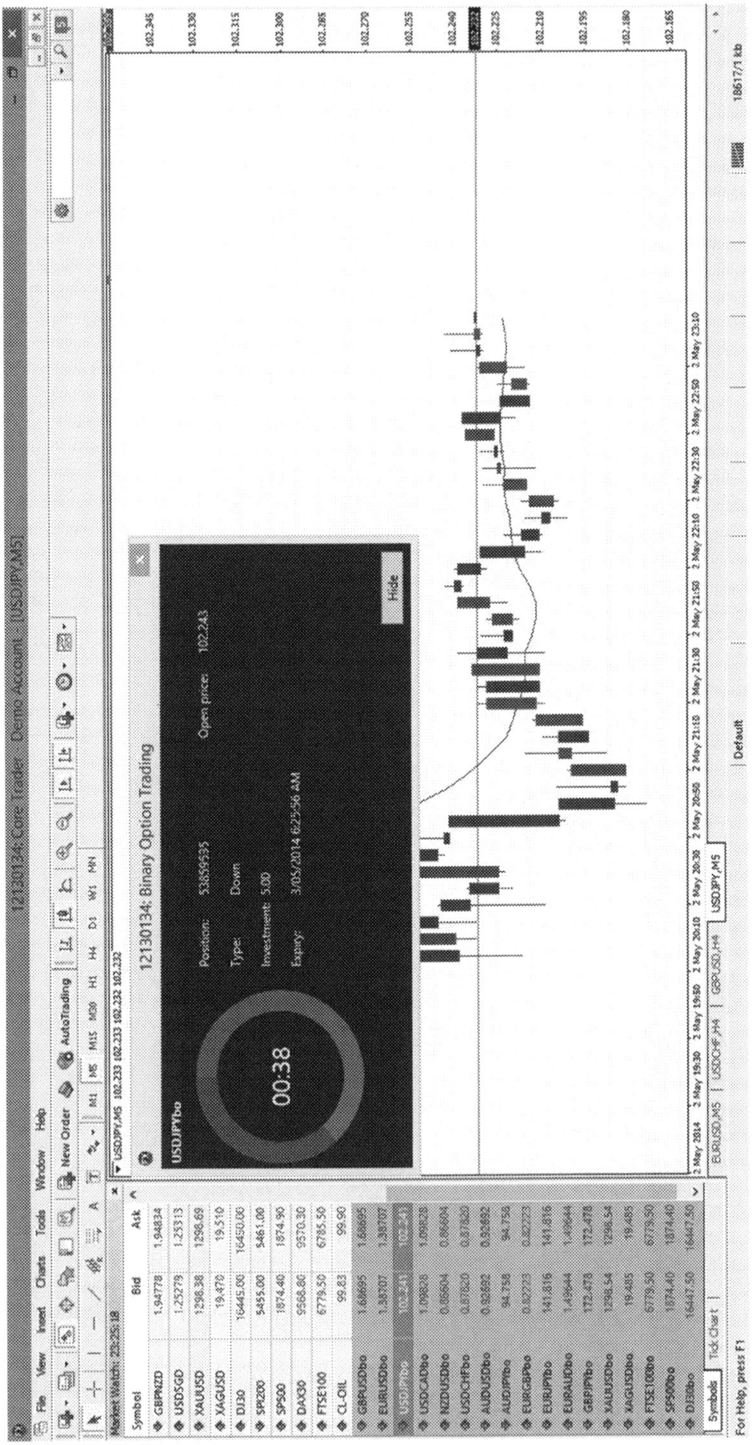

Figure 33: A binary options trade in progress on CLM Forex platform.

That concludes our set-up of the trading platform and chart window for the three brokers in discussion. We will go trading soon. Please note that setting up the desktop for trading is entirely your choice as you may have preference for one way or the other in terms of window sizing and positioning. Please do experiment with the best desktop arrangement that you feel comfortable with by positioning and sizing the two windows. Irrespective of whatever arrangement you settle with, please make sure that you are able to see a sizeable part of the chart window as critical trading decisions are going to be based on the price action only visible in the chart window. And once you are ready to place the trade, you are able to do so without any need to switch windows and wasting time in the process. The above, of course, applies only for the IG Markets and Stockpair trading platforms. CLM, on the other hand, is an all-inclusive chart and trading window, so there is no such requirement as in the case of other two platforms.

— **End of Chapter 8** —

CHAPTER 9

Putting All These Together: Looking for Set-Up

Now that we have learnt what are we going to do to earn a daily income and have set up the desktop to start to get into action, let me remind you one thing before you click on the Submit button or take the trade. I couldn't overemphasize the importance of discipline, perseverance, belief, and purpose in whatever you do—be it trading or anything else you have ventured into doing. You may have the best trading skill and strategy, but without having a trained mind that can handle successes and failures alike, you will have occasional success and not the sustained one. So please pay attention to this thought, and go over Chapter 7 again and again if you need to.

So we have got our desktop organized to start trading. We are mentally prepared to do so. Let's look at what are we looking for in a chart before we take a trade.

Please note that, irrespective of whichever platform you are trading on, your trading decision will be based on your reading of the chart. Go back to the charting window and have a look at it in terms of the confluence of three different situations lining up; *confluence* means 'occurring at the same time'. The three situations I am talking about are:

1. Is the price of the instrument EURUSD near a support or resistance line?

2. At the same instant and as the five-minute candle closes, what is the shape of the candle, is that a doji or hammer or a hanging man or inverted hammer?

3. At that instant, where is the stochastic oscillator located? Is it near the 20% or 80% mark?

Let me explain the confluence of the above three situations and how we make our decision to enter a trade based on that. First, as I have emphasized in Chapter 6, support and resistance lines are always important areas from where the price bounces back. Please remember, there is a strong chance that the price will bounce from that line, but there is also a smaller chance that the price will go through the support or resistance line. Is there a way to be absolutely sure whether or not the price is going to bounce back or go through support and resistance lines? Unfortunately, no, as we have no idea how the market is going to behave in such short time frames. But the good news is that there is another tool that might give us a confirmation or at least a better indication of whether or not the price is going to bounce back or pierce through. And that is the candlestick.

As mentioned, the candlestick provides insight on what traders are thinking or doing. We will know that from the shape of the candle. So if we see a candle where there is price rejection, that might give us an indication of the next possible movement of the price.

As mentioned in Chapter 5, any candle that has a long wick either at the bottom or at the top and has a body less than about one-third of the total length of the candle would be called a candle with price rejection. Please go back to Chapter 5 for candlestick patterns. The hammer, hanging-man, and shooting-star candles would fall in this category. These types of candles indicate that prices tend to close at the other end while rejecting the prices at the end where there is a long wick.

So far, we saw the confluence of support and resistance lines with rejection candles to get a possible idea of the price movement in the next time frame. But is there any other way we could find out how much pressure is being created in the market for the price to move in the direction that we thought it would? The answer to this question can be found by looking at the stochastic indicator. If the stochastic indicator is either above 80% or below 20%, then it gives us a further indication of pressure being created in the market. The oversold situation with stochastic indicator below the 20% line means that the pressure is for the price to move upwards. Similarly, the overbought situation with stochastic indicator above the 80% line means that pressure is being created in the market for the price to move downwards.

As mentioned a few times in this book, we are working on the statistical probability, and we would like to maximize the possibility of making the right decision using a variety of tools and by checking the confluence of three parameters as mentioned above. Let's look at the possible scenarios, following which we will go through case studies so that we feel comfortable to take our trades.

For the purpose of clarity, if you are trading with the expectation that the price is going to go above your current price or the closing price of the trade is going to be higher than the price at which you entered into the trade, then you would be expecting that the combination of the candles—either all *bull* or a mix of *bull* and *bear*—formed in the next 15 or 20 minutes (depending upon the expiry time you are using based on the broker's platform) is such that the closing price of the third/fourth candle is higher than the current price of EURUSD. Similarly, if you entered into a trade with the expectation that the price is going to go below your current price or the closing price of the trade is going to be lower than the price at which you entered into the trade, then you would be expecting that the combination of candles—either all *bear* or a mix of *bear* and *bull*—formed in the next 15 or 20 minutes is such that the closing price of the third/fourth candle is lower than the current price of EURUSD.

Note that, for all future trading examples we will use 20 minutes expiry. The same concept applies also for 15 minute expiry. The difference is that, since you are trading off 5 minute chart, we are looking at four candles after the set-up candle for the trade to expire whereas you would be looking at three candles for 15 minute expiry as each candle is of 5 minute worth of time.

Since we are looking for EURUSD to either be *up/above* or *down/below* the price at which we enter into a trade, let's look only at the scenarios in which price has a strong probability of moving in the two directions—*up* or *down*.

Let us name the two scenarios as follows for ease of comprehension and reference:

Scenario 1: Setups for EURUSD price to move higher, and
Scenario 2: Setups for EURUSD price to move lower

Set-Up for the Price to Go Up/Above

In this section, we are going to look for setup scenarios where the EURUSD price is expected to move higher from the current price in next 20 minutes.

The price of the EURUSD will have a very high probability to move upward in next 20 minutes or at the close of four 5-minute candles if...

1.   a hammer candle is formed in a downtrend,
2.   near a *support* line and
3.   the stochastic indicator is near or below 20% line,

So we are looking at these three conditions to be met before we decide to enter into a trade.

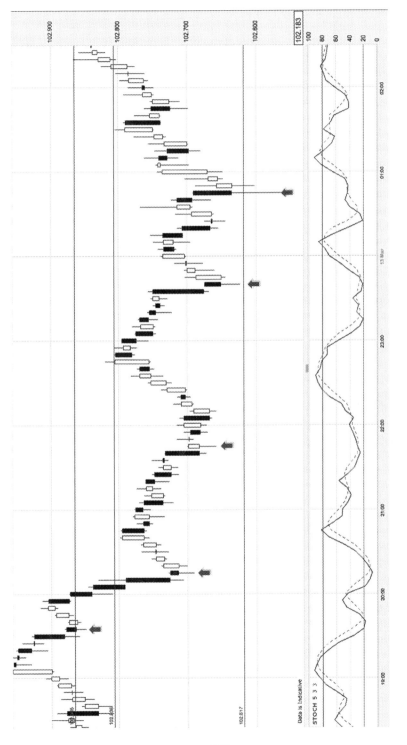

Figure 34: Scenario 1, set-up 1: EURUSD to be *above* the current value.

Refer to Figure 34 for an explanation of how the trade set-up happens. Looking at the leftmost arrow, you could see that there is a hammer candle near the support line, and the stochastic indicator was close to the 20% line. This means that the three conditions mentioned above have been met. As such, we expect the price to bounce back, and so it does as the hammer candle is followed by three *bull* candles and one *bear* candle in the next 20 minutes. So if you enter a trade and choose the option for the price to go *above* the current price, you would have won the trade. Let's call this *scenario 1, set-up 1.*

While the above defines an ideal situation, you are unlikely to come across too many of those in any given period of time. In order to give ourselves little more opportunities to trade to ensure to keep up with the statistical probabilities, let us look at possible variations.

Variation 1 to the scenario 1 set-up: *bear hammer candle.* The type of the price rejection candle adds to the probability of the price moving higher. My observation is that if the price rejection candle is a *bear* hammer candle in the scenario 1 above, I would be more comfortable to take the trade. This is simply for the reason that with a bear price rejection candle, there is larger room for the price to move up, thus giving us a higher probability for the trade to succeed. Let's call this *scenario 1, set-up 2.*

Variation 2 to the scenario 1 set-up: *bear candle with a small wick.* As mentioned above, we are looking for a *bear* hammer candle near the *support* line, which is our indication to enter into a trade. But there are situations where you might see a large *bear* candle with a wick at the bottom or at the top which is about one-third to half of the total length of the candle. If such a candle is formed near the *support* line, there is a strong probability of the price to move up in the next few timeframes. I cannot assign a probability of the price moving up with this set-up, but I would certainly recommend that you study the historical patterns in the chart and see how often this set-up happens and what the corresponding result is. Let us call it *scenario 1, set-up 3.*

Variation 3 to the scenario 1 set-up: *doji candle.* You might also come across situations where a doji candle is formed near the support line, and you might be tempted to take a trade. Although you might end up being a winner, personally, I have low confidence in the doji candle as a reversal candle. Doji by definition is indecisiveness, and hence, the price could move in either direction following the formation of a doji candle. But some traders do think that doji is a sign of reversal, and price would retrace following a doji candle. However, if it is a dragonfly doji in a downtrend, I would be more comfortable in taking the trade primarily because the dragonfly doji signifies lower price rejection; the *bulls* are pushing the price up, and hence, closing price of the doji is on the high side of the candle. Let us call it *scenario 1, set-up 4.*

Variation 4 to the scenario 1 set-up: *spinning-top candle.* Often a spinning-top candle, either *bear* or *bull*, near the *support* line is a good indication of the price to move up. My observation is that the probability of the price to move up with a spinning top is almost the same as the probability of a *bear* hammer candle—in other words, fairly high confidence. Let us call it *scenario 1, set-up 5.*

Variation 5 to the scenario 1 set-up: *inverted-hammer candle.* As mentioned in the chapter on candlesticks, the inverted-hammer candle also represents a strong probability of reversal. So look for formation of an inverted-hammer candle near the support line for possible reversal in the price and corresponding formation of a series of *bull* candles in the next few timeframes. I personally do not have very strong confidence in inverted-hammer candle for taking a trade, but as you study the chart more over a longer period of time, you will be able to make a better decision of whether or not you would trade in this set-up. Let us call it *scenario 1, set-up 6.*

So in summary, for us to take a trade where we would expect the price to move higher, we are looking for a set-up consisting of the following criteria:

1. There is a downtrend with an appropriate candle formed—best if it is a *bear* hammer candle or dragonfly doji.
2. Current price is near a *support* line.
3. *Stochastic* indicator is near or below the 20% line.

Let's now have a look at a few case studies and take a look at a real EURUSD five-minute chart to see whether or not the set-ups described above will deliver the result we are aiming for.

Let us look at Figure 35. clearly, it is the type of set-up we would like to have all the time. As you can see, this is a clear winner, with three bull candles and one bear candle forming after the set-up candle and the closing price being significantly higher than the opening price, something like a textbook set-up. There is no hesitation in taking the trade—pure cash equivalent!

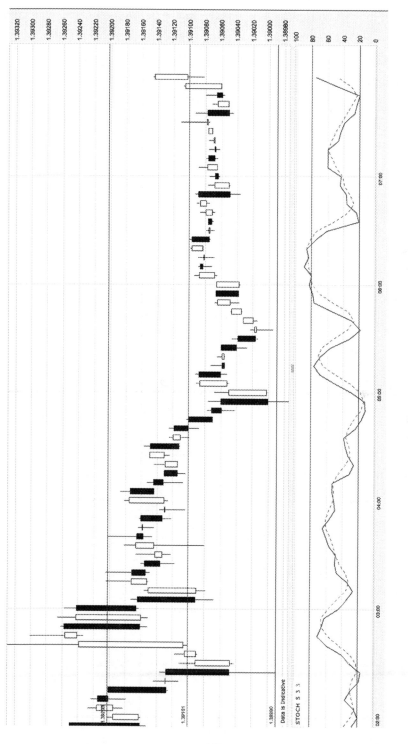

Figure 35: Scenario 1, typical set-up.

Figure 36 shows another few set-ups where the probability of success is very high, and as you can see, all of those were clear winners as the following candles after the set-up candle turned out to be mix of *bull* and *bear* candles such that the closing price was much higher than the opening price.

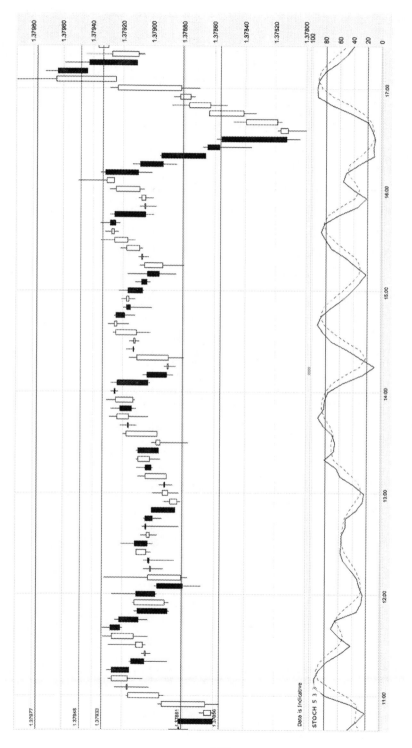

Figure 36: Scenario 1, set-up 1: another example of a typical high-probability set-up.

I am giving several other examples to illustrate the set-up you would see where you would expect the price to go *above* the current price. I would suggest you look at the chart on your computer. See for yourself all these variations of set-up, and make yourself comfortable with the ideal set-up with which you would feel confident to trade. Let me remind you again, you are playing a game of statistics in which you are improving your batting average by sticking to the set-up and its variations as described in this chapter and being successful more than at least 55% of the time.

Scenario 1, set-up 2: *bear hammer candle*. Figure 37 in the following page shows some examples of scenario 1, set-up 2, where we are looking for a *bear* hammer candle during a downtrend. Please see the arrow on the left. The *bear* hammer candle is a clear winner as the following candle is a *bull* candle followed by more *bull* candles as the closing price after 20 minutes is way higher than the price at which you would have taken the trade. Same for the *bull* hammer candle in the right arrow, that trade was also a clear winner. Please note that the following candle after the hammer is a bear candle but the price did reverse in the following two candles as those two are bull candles. Although, the two bull candles were followed by a bear candle, the closing price of the bear candle at the end of the 20 minute trade was higher than the opening price of the trade. So you win again.

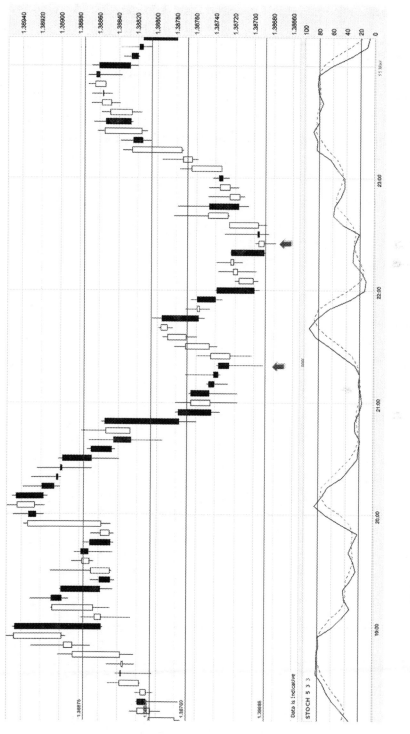

Figure 37: Scenario 1, set-up 2: winners with *bear* and *bull* hammer candles.

More examples of scenario 1, set-up 2 are in Figure 38. Please do study the charts and familiarize yourself with the variations of the set-ups. In the example below on the left, the hammer has a much longer shadow and very small body—a hammer nonetheless. Pay particular attention to the shape of the hammer. You may not always expect to see a perfect hammer with no or very short wick on the top. But the more perfect the hammer is, the higher is the probability of success of the trade. Sometimes a candlestick may have a relatively longer wick on top but still shorter compared to the bottom wick, almost looking like a hammer candle. Double-check the shape of the candle before entering into a trade.

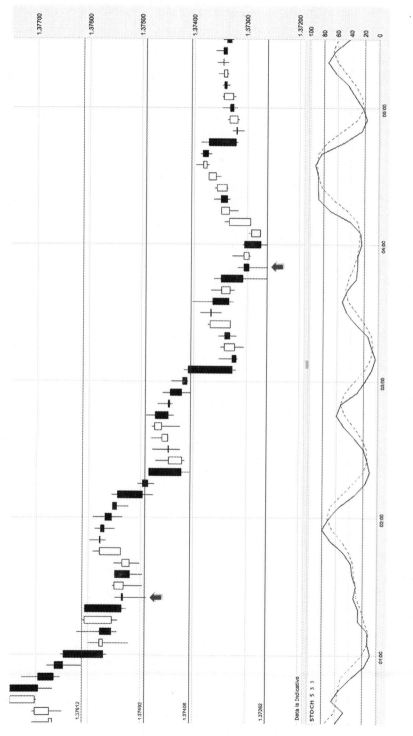

Figure 38: Scenario 1, set-up 2: more examples of the winners with *bear* hammer candle.

Scenario 1, set-up 3: *bear candle with longer bottom wicks*. Figure 39 shows some examples of this set-up. The set-ups are marked with arrows. You might notice that a lower price rejection is the main clue for you as *bulls* are pushing the price up, and here is your chance to go with the *bulls* and pull the trigger. The stochastic oscillator may be a very important indicator as described before, but you have confluence of two indications in the chart in Figure 39 that the lower price rejection candle formed near a support line.

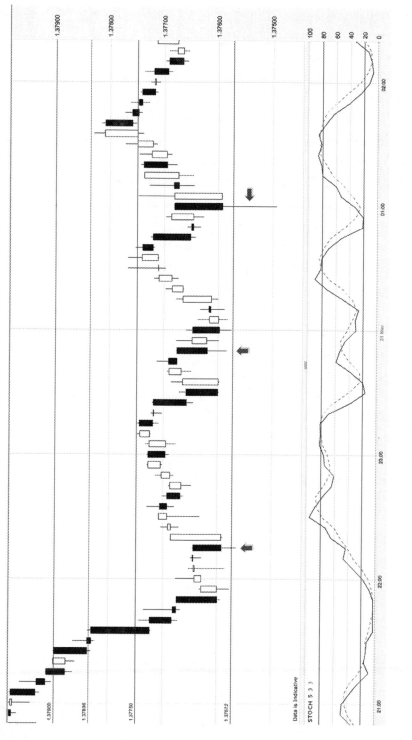

Figure 39: Scenario 1, set-up 3: *bear* candle with longer bottom wicks near a support line.

Generally, I prefer to take the trade where the short-term downtrend has at least two *bear* candles as in the middle arrow of Figure 39. But if the *bear* candle touches the support line and close above it, then I would think it is worthwhile to consider taking the trade, as in the arrow on the left of the chart at Figure 39 and also the arrow on the right of the chart. And both turned out to be winners with price at the close is higher than the closing price of the set-up candle. The set-up candle in the middle, however, was looking right but the trade turned out to be a loser as you might have noticed that the closing price of the fourth candle was lower than the closing price of the set-up candle.

Make sure that the support line is drawn correctly as the price reversal takes place near the support line. The candle is the indication of whether or not the market direction is turning in the direction you think it is going. The lower price rejection near the support line is the key for you to get into the trade. What was stochastic oscillator doing at that time? Ideally, the stochastic oscillator should be near or below the 20% line, but even if it is not so, you might be able to enter a trade as long as the stochastic oscillator is not close to the overbought line of 80%. In Figure 39, the two *bear* candles on the left are formed while the stochastic oscillator is at about the 50% mark, which is not quite near 20%, but as you can see, the trades would have been a winner if you had taken those trades.

Scenario 1, set-up 4: *doji candle*. As mentioned before, I am not fully comfortable to trade with a common doji candle simply because it is hard to determine if the price is going to reverse after a common doji.

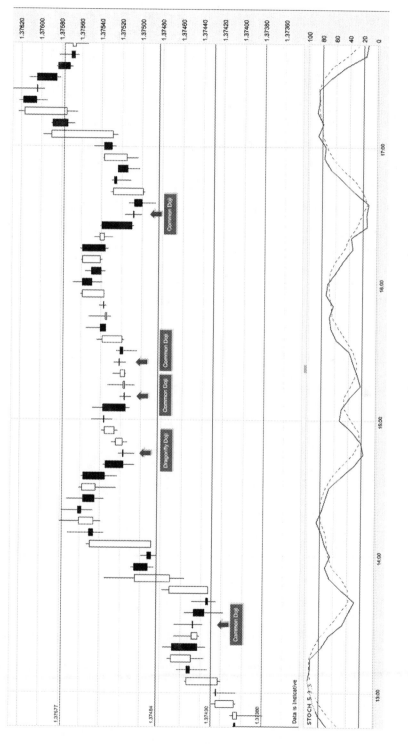

Figure 40: Scenario 1, set-up 4: possible set-up with common doji and dragonfly doji.

171

The candlestick chart in Figure 40 shows examples of the common doji as well as the dragonfly doji in a live chart. Some of the common doji candle set-ups in the chart would be winners and some losers. So I would think that the reliability of the doji as a signal for price reversal is perhaps very low. It is up to the traders with experience to know whether you will be able to make decisions on whether or not you would take trades with a doji, but keeping statistical probability in mind, the dragonfly doji can help improve your probability of success.

Scenario 1, set-up 5: *spinning-top candle.* Spinning-top candle offers good probability of reversal if the candle is *bull* in a downtrend or *bear* in an uptrend. The confidence level in spinning-top candle as a sign of reversal is generally very high and offers some great opportunities to enter into a trade.

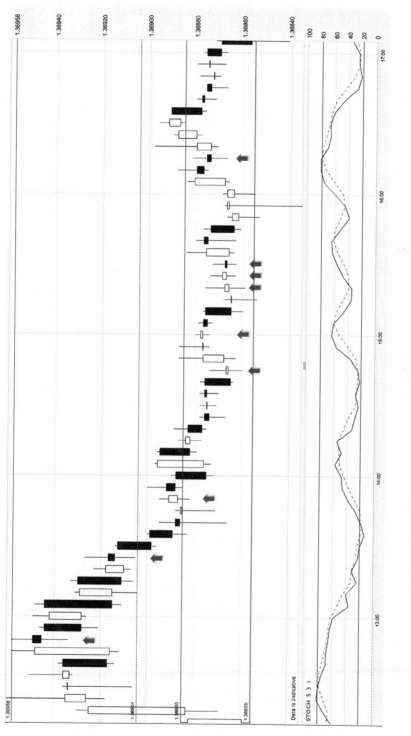

Figure 41: Scenario 1, set-up 5: trade set-up with spinning-top candle.

173

In Figure 41, some of the trades would have been winner and some losers. Please note that there are times during which the trading activities in the market tend to slow down for a variety of reasons, ranging from lunch break to the calm before the release of a major report on economic events. At such times, the market tends to move sideways, the resulting candles formed take the shape of doji candles to spinning tops, and the market will seem to lack a sense of direction. The three spinning tops in the middle of the chart seem to be a period of low activity, causing the market to almost stall, and traders are advised to avoid trading around those times of the day. You would like the market to be range-bound and moving for you to take the trade not while the market is moving sideways.

Scenario 1, set-up 6: *inverted-hammer candle.* Figure 42 shows some examples of an inverted hammer in a live chart. The shape of the inverted hammer may vary, and hence, I have included a few examples so that you will get to know the candle in a real environment as and when such a candle is formed.

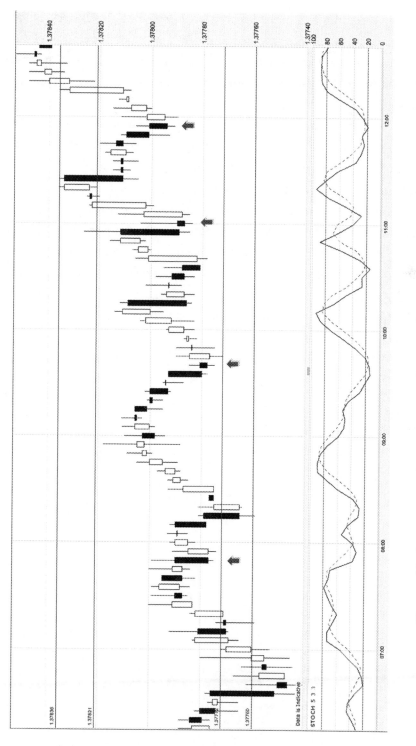

Figure 42: Scenario 1, set-up 6: examples of an inverted hammer in a live chart.

175

In a live trading situation, keeping an eye on the candlestick is very important as the price keeps moving and the candlestick is being drawn on your chart. Watch for the longer upper wick for an early indication of the inverted-hammer candlestick, and watch if the closing price is not too far from the opening price.

The inverted-hammer candle is fairly reliable if the closing price is near a support line. I would feel comfortable to take a trade with an inverted-hammer candle if the candle is in a downtrend with at least two or three *bear* (red) candles in a row and, of course, near a support line. The *bear* inverted-hammer candle means that there is some room for the price to retrace similar to a regular *bear* hammer candle. As always, please be familiarized by going back from time to time and looking at candlestick charts for more inverted-hammer candles and seeing for yourself how and when such candles are formed and whether or not the following candle is a *bull* candle as you would be expecting the price to move up after an inverted-hammer candle.

Set-Up for the Price to Go Down/Below

In this section, we are going to look at the set-ups that will help us make decision about whether the price of the asset is going below the current price based on the technical analysis.

The price of the EURUSD will have a very high probability to move lower in next 20 minutes or at the close of four 5-minute candles if...

1. a shooting-star candle is formed in an uptrend,
2. near a *resistance* line and
3. the stochastic oscillator is near or above the 80% line

Please refer to Figure 43 for an example of what it looks like to have the confluence of the three parameters above.

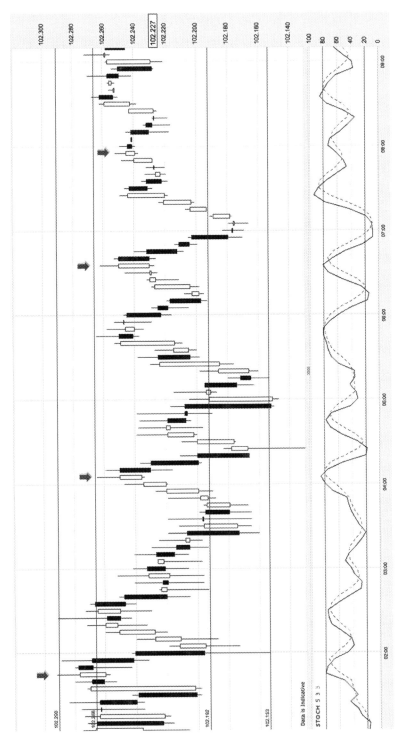

Figure 43: Scenario 2, set-up 1: EURUSD to be *below* the current value.

178

This is very similar to scenario 1 except that we are looking for the value of the EURUSD to move *below* the current value in the next 20-minute time frame, so in essence, scenario 2 is a reverse of scenario 1 in many respects. Let's call this basic set-up as scenario 2, set-up 1.

In order for us to make sure such trading set-up works for us and that there are more opportunities to trade, let us explore possible variations of the set-up.

Variation 1 to scenario 2, set-up 1: *bull* shooting-star candle. Similar to scenario 1, the colour of the price rejection candle adds to the probability of the price moving lower. If it is a *bull* shooting-star candle in the scenario 2 above, I would be more comfortable to take the trade. This is simply for the reason that with a *bull* price rejection candle, there is a larger room for the price to move downwards, thus giving us a higher probability for the trade to succeed.

Let's look at Figure 43. All the shooting-star candles are *bull*, and all trades, if taken on closing of those *bull* candles, would have turned out to be winners. There is also a *bear* shooting-star candle unmarked in between the two arrows in the middle of the chart. That trade also turned out to be a winner as price did move downwards following the close of the candle. Just to reiterate, since you are taking a trade with 20-minute expiry, you would be looking for the closing value of EURUSD at the close of the fourth candle after you have taken the trade. Let's call this scenario 2, set-up 2.

Variation 2 to the scenario 2 set-up: *bull* candle with small wick. As mentioned above, we are looking for a *bull* shooting-star candle near the *resistance* line, which is our indication to enter into a trade. But there are situations where you might see a large *bull* candle with a wick at the top which is about one-third to half of the total length of the candle. If such a candle is formed near the *resistance* line, there is a strong probability of the price to move down in the next time frame. I cannot assign a probability of the price moving up with this set-up, but I would certainly recommend that you study the historical patterns in the chart and see how often this set-up happens and what the corresponding result in the following candles are. Let us call it scenario 2, set-up 3.

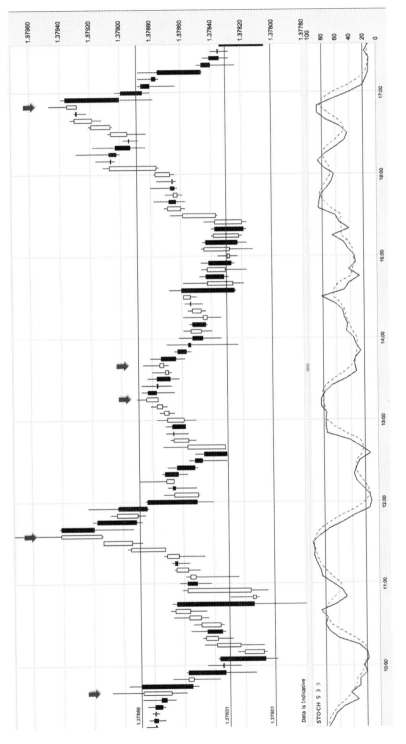

Figure 44: Bull candle with small wick at the top.

180

Variation to the scenario 2 set-up: spinning-top candle. A spinning-top candle, either *bear* or *bull*, in an uptrend near the *resistance* line with stochastic oscillator near or above the 80% line is a good set-up, and it would be expected that the price of EURUSD will move *below* the current price in the next 20-minute time frame. Please see Figure 45 for some examples of such a set-up. Please note that the spinning-top candle do not occur that frequently, and you may not be able to see too many during normal trading hours unless the market is moving sideways during a thin trading period. Spinning-top candles may be in a range of shapes—some with long wicks at both ends, some with very short wicks, some with relatively larger bodies, and so on.

Spinning-top candle is a variation of the doji except that it has a slightly larger body than doji. As such, the reliability of the spinning-top candle as a trade set-up is often similar to that of a doji candle and lower than that of a *bull* shooting star in an uptrend. Let us call it scenario 2, set-up 4.

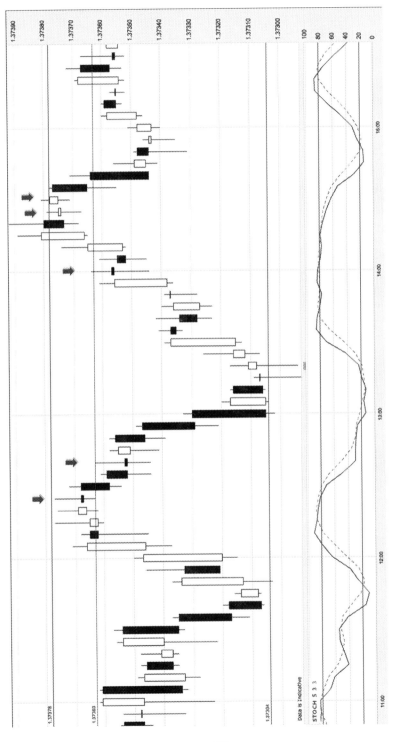

Figure 45: Scenario 2, set-up 4: spinning-top candles in an uptrend.

In Figure 45, trades taken following the leftmost spinning-top candle would have been a winner and so are the two rightmost spinning-top candles. But the trades taken following the two middle spinning-top candles would have been losers as EURUSD did turn around immediately following the spinning-top candles but not after 20-minute expiry time. But as you gather more experience with trading, you will be able to make the right call of whether or not you are comfortable to trade with spinning-top candles.

Variation to the scenario 2 set-up: doji candle. You might also come across situations where a doji candle is formed near the support line, and you might be tempted to take a trade. Although you might end up being a winner, personally, I have low confidence in the doji candle as a reversal candle. Doji, by definition, is indecisiveness, and hence, the price could move in either direction following the formation of a doji candle. But some traders do think that doji is a sign of reversal, and price would retrace following a doji candle. Let us call it scenario 2, set-up 5.

So in summary, for us to take a trade where we would expect the price to move lower or for us to choose *below* on the trading platform, we are looking at a set-up consisting of the following criteria:

1. There is an uptrend with an appropriate candle formed, preferably a shooting-star or a *bull* candle with a small top wick.
2. Current value is near a *resistance* line.
3. *Stochastic* oscillator is near or above the 80% line.

In this section, I have described the two scenarios in which the value of EURUSD may be *above* or *below* the current value or the value at which you would have entered in a trade. Please note that in a typical trading day, you will come across both scenarios in a variety of combinations. You will have to make a decision whether to enter into a trade, keeping in mind the set-ups you will see near the *support* and *resistance* lines. So the key is to keep an eye when the EURUSD value is close to either of the two lines.

Set-ups on a Typical Trading Day

Let us look at a typical trading day and see for ourselves how many trading set-ups you are likely to come across and how many of those set-ups would be winners. You will appreciate that not all days are the same and that some days may have more trading opportunities than the others. Please refer to Figure 46 in the following page and it appears that you could potentially have six trading setups as shown in the chart. Let us discuss each of the setups in little details, starting from the left most arrow.

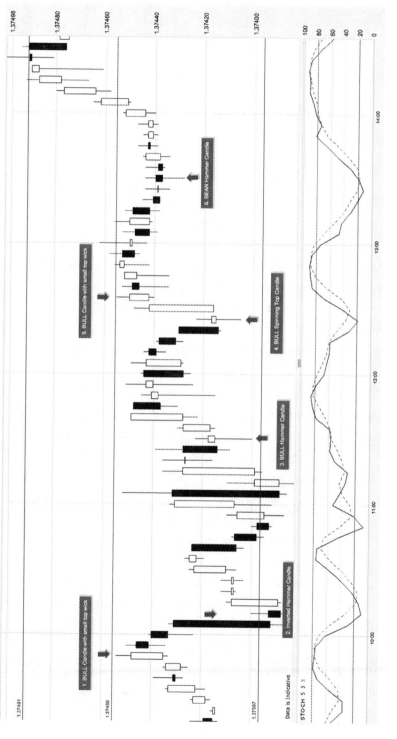

Figure 46: Set-ups on a typical trading day.

1. *Bull* candle with a top wick: This candle is formed just before 10 a.m. AEST or before the stock market opens in Australia. The *bull* candle with a small wick is the set-up for the price to move *below* the closing price of the candle in the next 20 minutes. The price smoothly fell below the closing price of the *bull* candle as it was followed by three *bear* candles. This is a clear winner.

2. Inverted-hammer candle: This is a set-up for the price to move *above* the closing price of the inverted-hammer candle. Price did move upwards as the set-up candle was followed by a large *bull* candle and three more candles, with the 20-minute trade closing well above the opening price. This is also a winner.

3. *Bull* hammer candle: This is the so-called bread-and-butter set-up for the price to move upwards. The *bull* hammer candle is formed during a downtrend and is close to a *support* line, so you would expect the price to move up. Trades taken on closing of the candle would have resulted in a winner as you can see from the chart that in the next 20 minutes, the price had moved significantly upwards with three *bull* candles and one small *bear* candle in between. This is also a clear winner.

4. *Bull* spinning-top candle: On this day, we had so far three winning trades, so we may feel that our risk appetite might be a little higher than if it was the first trade of the day. Although spinning-top candle set-up does not necessarily have a high confidence of success, we might be inclined to take the trade. If you did take the trade, on the close of the *bull* spinning top at the fourth arrow from the left, it appears that the price did move higher with the formation of three *bull* candles and one *bear* candle immediately following the spinning-top candle. As it turns out, this is also a winner.

5. *Bull* candle with a top wick: While the trade taken on the close of the *bull* spinning-top candle is still on or the 20 minutes has not yet expired since taking the trade, there seems to be another trading opportunity with the formation of a *bull* candle with a top wick 15 minutes into the previous trade. You may be inclined to take that trade as well as this set-up candle is formed near the *resistance* line and the stochastic oscillator is also very close to the 80% line. If you decide

to take that trade with the expectation of the price to move lower in the next 20 minutes, then your decision would have resulted in a winner. Look at the candles formed immediately following the *bull* candle with a top wick, the price did move downwards in the next five-minute candle, followed by a move upwards with two more *bull* candles after the set-up candle. But the last five-minute candle turned out to be a *bear* candle, making the closing price just lower than our opening price. This means that by the skin of the teeth, this trade also is a winner.

6. *Bear* hammer candle: This is also similar to the third trade with the *bull* hammer candle except that the candle is *bear*, meaning this has higher confidence compared to the *bull* hammer candle trade. Looking at the chart, note that the candle is not near the *support* line we had drawn, but there is confluence of two other parameters. First, it is a *bear* hammer candle in a downtrend, which means that there is a lower price rejection with possibility of price being pushed up. Second, the stochastic oscillator is near about or below the 20% line, which means the market seems to be oversold and it is time for the *bulls* to step in to push the price higher. This seems to be a good set-up for the price to move higher, and so it did. The *bear* hammer set-up candle is followed by a combination of *bull* and *bear* candles, but the price did end up closing higher than the closing price of the set-up candle. So if you would have taken the trade on the closing of the *bear* hammer candle, you would have been a winner.

So it seems we had a great day so far; we had identified six set-ups in a typical trading day between 10 a.m. and 4 p.m. AEST, and all the trades, if taken, would have turned out to be winners.

So going back to Tool No. 5 on Chapter 6, which is on having a plan, if you had invested $50 per trade, you would have earned a profit of $243 by the end of the trading session of the day. That is very close to the $250 a day that we had planned to achieve. If you had invested $100 a trade, the end of the day profit would have been $486 and so on. So you can see for yourself the potential daily income from a very simple trading technique.

Please always bear in mind that you are working with probabilities. The tools suggested in this book increase your chances to have better than 50% probability of success—sometimes even 100% as in the example trading day discussed above. But all the trading days may not be as good as this, and you will have varied percentages of success on any given day depending on various situations that's beyond anyone's reasonable control. But that's where our probability kicks in, and over a given period of time (say, daily or weekly or even monthly), we would like to achieve a minimum of 60% successful trades—the higher the better. If you can avoid being in trade on highly volatile days, such as when there is big economic news or news affecting some of the largest economies of the world, you will do well and have much higher success.

In my experiences of trading for quite a long time now, I have noticed that the market may behave quite irrationally on occasions. As an example, you would have taken a trade based on a perfect set-up, but because of sudden changes in the trading environment, the price collapses on you, and the price moves in the completely opposite direction, resulting in a loss in an otherwise very winnable trade. The opposite also happens like when you would take a trade with not much confidence and the price would make a large move in your favour for no apparent reason and your trade would turn out to be a winner. This is where the probability mindset comes handy. You will win some and lose some. The idea is to keep more winners than losers so that you have a net profit after accounting for the losses.

— **End of Chapter 9** —

CHAPTER 10

Putting All These Together: Placing the Trade

So far, we have discussed all the tools we need to start the trading and under what conditions we are ready to enter into a trade or if there is a set-up. Once we are satisfied that there is a set-up as mentioned in the previous chapter either in scenario 1 or scenario 2, we are now ready to place a trade. This is where the rubber meets the road as we actually invest our real money in expectation of a profit. The procedures to place a trade varies from platform to platform, but I have covered three very different styles of platforms so that you can understand what to look for and where before you place your first trade.

Please note that IG Markets' sprint market platform is a different type of platform compared to that of Stockpair in a sense that most of the binary-options-only brokers have platforms very similar to Stockpair except for some minor variations in the look and feel. CLM's binary-options platform, on the contrary, is an even more different type of platform. So with these three platforms covered, you should feel reasonably comfortable to trade with any other broker's platform. Please do review Tool No. 3 in Chapter 6, which is on brokers, before you open an account with any of these brokers.

Let's look at all the three platforms, but before we place the trade, let me remind you that timing is everything, and here is why.

Since we are looking at a five-minute chart, the decision to take a trade will happen within any block of five minutes. If you happen to make a decision to take a trade, that will have to happen pretty much right on the dot, just before the next five-minute block starts, or as soon as possible, around the time the next candlestick opens. So you will need to get fully prepared with all other settings, depending upon the trading platform you are using. And you will need to keep an eye on the clock, so your multitasking skill may be called into action in some ways as described below.

In Chapter 8, the section on setting up the trading platform, you have already learnt what the various parameters are in both the platforms and how to set them up. We will not revisit those, but I have to say, please confirm that all parameters are appropriately set on the platform before you start trading. Those parameters include market, premium, expiry, and direction. Once these are set, you are ready to trade.

Sprint Markets' Platform

IG Markets' sprint markets are a very different class of platform, but it is very simple to put a trade after you have set all the parameters as described before. With the candlestick chart in the background, you will need to keep an eye on the specific candle that you would consider as a set-up candle based on what we have learnt so far. While you are watching the candle, you are also going to keep an eye on the clock right below the line chart in the trading platform window. This is the main clock based on which the candles are formed. So as the clock counts up and comes to the end of the five-minute block, such as 10.25, you will click on the Submit button on the right to enter into the trade.

Would you be looking at the chart all along during the trading hours? Well, that's an option, but I don't think that's the best utilization of your time. Secondly, the purpose of this whole exercise is for you to have more quality time for yourself and not be at sitting in front of your computer, staring at the monitor like being in a job where you need to be at a certain place at a certain time for the full duration of the day. So how do you do that? Please go back to Chapter 8, where I had mentioned about the timer on your iPhone or something similar. Set the timer so that you get an alert about 40 to 45 seconds before every 5 minutes. Keep the alert device close to you so that you hear the alert loud and clear as it is important that you give yourself the maximum possible chance to trade every good set-up.

So when the alert goes off, please go back to the screen of your computer and see if the current EURUSD price is anywhere close to the *support* or *resistance* line. If not, go back to what you were doing, maybe reading a book or watching a movie or maybe playing with your young child. If yes, see if the candlestick in the current five-minute block near the support or resistance line is one that you are looking for—such as a hammer, shooting star, and so on and so forth—as required for a good set-up.

If the set-up is good and you have decided to put on a trade, then move the cursor on the Submit button. As the clock counts up in the next 40 to 45 seconds based on your timer alert and reaches the top of 5 minutes, such as 10.25, click on the Submit button to enter into a trade. Voila, you are in a trade, and hope it goes in your favour. I hear you ask, if I can't click Submit exactly on the top of five-minute block, am I not able to enter into a trade? The answer is, you can enter into a trade at any time, but the expiry will count from there. For example, if you enter into a trade with 20-minute expiry at 10.25.05 hours, the trade will expire at 10.45.05 hours.

The whole purpose of entering into a trade at the top of the five-minute block is that, with the five-minute candlestick chart, each candle represents a five-minute time frame, and the candles start and close at the top of every five minutes. Having said that, with your trading time frame aligned with that of the candlestick chart, you can take the most advantage on your trading decisions based on a fully completed candle rather than having to make a decision halfway through the formation of the candle. So unless you have a valid reason to do otherwise, please do try to take the trade at the top of the five-minute block. But if for some reason you clicked a few seconds early or late, that's OK too as long as it is not a minute away or a minute early.

Stockpair's Platform

Key aspects of placing the trade remain the same with the sprint markets platform, except that the parameters of interest are named differently. So with Stockpair's platform, we are looking at presetting the asset which, in this case, is EURUSD, selected from the left of the screen. Stockpair platform do not offer a 20-minute expiry, so we will go with the 15-minute expiry selected from the pull-down menu right below the main question 'Will EUR/USD go up or down?' You will choose the direction with the arrow buttons on the two sides of the instrument name, which is EURUSD in this case. The fourth parameter to set is the amount of investment for the trade. This is set through the Set Your Trade box on the right, and you will enter $50 here as per the plan. If you would like to start with a smaller amount, you can enter the amount in the box.

With all these parameters preset, you can enter a trade just by clicking the big button on the right called Buy. By clicking the button and confirming the order, you will enter into the trade. But that's after Chapter 9. When we see our set-up, we will click Buy.

CLM's Platform

As mentioned a few times in this book, the trading and charting platforms on CLM are one and the same, and you can access both from one single screen. This is a good advantage compared to that of IG Markets and Stockpair, where you will need to work with two different screens for decision-making and placing the order.

To place an order on the CLM platform, please find the asset from the Market Watch window on the left. You are going to pick EURUSDbo as this is the binary option version of the asset EURUSD, which is traded as spot forex. Double-click on EURUSDbo, and it will open up a small window for trading binary options. You will need to set only the investment amount and the expiry to enter into the trade. You will need to enter the investment amount in a white box marked 'Amount'.

In our example, we are going to enter $50 in that box. Next, you pick the expiry time from the pull-down menu in the box marked 'Expiry'. As per our strategy, we are going to pick 20 minutes from the pull-down menu under the expiry option. That's all the setting you will need for entering into a trade. Once that is set, all you need to click is the up or down button on the same window to enter the trade. The platform does not ask for any further confirmation for entering into the trade.

Does that sound a little too overwhelming for you as you have to keep an eye on the candlestick chart, wait for the time alert to go off, and then click on the top of the five-minute block while keeping an eye on the clock? I guess it is possible that you would feel overwhelmed. But that's a very small price to pay for the daily income you are going to generate for yourself. Another good news is that IG Markets offers two weeks' trial or demo of trading on the platform with fake money. While opening your account, you can either start with a demo account, or you can have a real account with two weeks of trial. So you have ten working days to try out how to set up all these that we have discussed so far, including taking a trade. Once you feel comfortable with the set-ups and taking trades on the demo platform, you will be ready to place trades with the real-money account. With the real-money account, it is possible for your emotions to get in the way. If it does, please review Chapter 7, which is about the mind as your best tool, and you will feel more confident to take the trade.

Alternative Trading Time Frame

We have so far discussed the 5-minute candlestick chart and placing a trade with a 15- or 20-minute expiry. The whole reason behind this 5- or 20-minute trading is that on many occasions, the price does not necessarily turn around after you have a set-up. It may take another one or two candlesticks before the price goes in the direction that you thought it should be based on the set-up. This combination of the chart with a 5-minute time frame and the 20-minute expiry gives the trader the right ammunition to enter a trade with confidence as that has a proven success rate.

For some traders, the 5-minute time frame may be too short, and it may become difficult to follow the chart and place an order. So don't lose heart if you are one of those people. As such, I am offering an alternative, but this is in no way inferior trading than what we have learnt so far. As a matter of fact, the alternative may be somewhat better than that for a variety of reasons.

I am summarizing below some of the features of the alternative trading time frame:

1. Instead of a 5-minute chart, you will look at a 15-minute chart to make a decision to enter into a trade. Once you decide to enter a trade exactly as per the set-ups discussed in Chapter 9, you enter a trade with a 60-minute expiry of binary options.

2. A 60-minute expiry gives traders little more time to take the trade compared to a 20-minute expiry trade. Since prices generally move across a larger range in 60 minutes compared to 20 minutes, there is no need to place the trade immediately on the close of the 15-minute candle as you would have done if you were trading with a 5-minute chart with a 20-minute expiry.

3. Trading with a higher time frame often means trading with a reasonably defined market direction while trading with a lower time frame is often considered to be trading with noise or jitter in the market. This is the view of the proponents of higher-time-frame trading, and I think it is right to a large extent. However, a 15-minute chart with a 1-hour expiry is not quite a higher time frame—but only relatively— compared to trading with a 5-minute chart with a 20-minute expiry.

Last but not the least, for you to monitor the chart every 15 minutes, you will need a 15-minute timer similar to the one discussed in Chapter 9.

Complete Checklist for Trading

I like the concept of checklists or procedures used by airline pilots for everything they do before, after, and while flying a plane. I am one great fan of this as it establishes the steps for doing something beforehand in a mechanical way without having to think about the steps when a situation arises. So I am listing below the checklist for trading binary options, something that will ensure you are prepared.

1. Set up a 'trading' room or a place where you would have comfortable lighting with all physical tools for trading, such as computer, Internet connection, and timer.
2. Start the timer such that it goes off at least 40 seconds before the opening of the next candle.
3. Set up the EURUSD candlestick chart with the appropriate time frame based on the preferred trading style as discussed e.g. 5 minute chart for 15/20 minute expiry or 15 minute chart for 60 minute expiry.
4. Set up the trading platform as discussed in this chapter. The key parameters to remember and select are the following: asset to trade (EURUSD), the expiry time (20 or 15 minutes or 1 hour, depending upon your preference), the investment amount per trade, and the direction of the price movement of the asset (up/above or down/below).
5. Look for the set-ups after the timer goes off. You have 40 seconds to make a decision.
6. If a set-up exists, place a trade based on your assessment of the possible movement of the price.

Please do not forget to have some fun in the process.

— **End of Chapter 10** —

CHAPTER 11

Advanced Concepts in Trading Binary Options

I have included this chapter so that you are aware of some of the money management schemes traders often use to maximize the profits or turnaround of their trades. I thought your learning wouldn't be complete without knowing how to optimally manage your bankroll and trade successfully.

I have enumerated three schemes in this chapter. The first one is a proper money management system, which I would suggest you consider seriously using in your trading career. The other two are not strictly money management schemes as such, but your awareness of the schemes might help you at some stage of your trading career. I have used all three and will show you the results in the following chapters from my live trading statements.

Kelly's System

I have been working in the telecommunication industry for over 19 years, and if I hadn't brought in some references from the industry where I have worked that long, this book wouldn't have been completed! OK, on a serious note, of the various money management schemes that has been devised over the years to maximize the profit in trading, one is practised by large investment houses, and the credit goes to a gentleman named John Kelly.

John Kelly worked for AT&T's Bell Laboratories and built a mathematical model to assist AT&T with its long-distance telephone to minimize noise issues. After the method was published in scientific journals, the investing community realized its potential as an optimal money management system which has the ability to maximize the size of their bankroll over the long term. Today, many people use it as a general money management system for investing.

There are two basic components to the Kelly criterion. First is the win probability. This is the probability that any given trade you make will return a positive amount. The second component in the Kelly criterion is the ratio of wins to losses—the total positive trade amounts divided by the total negative trade amounts.

These two factors are then put into Kelly's equation:

$$\text{Kelly \%} = W - [(1 - W) / R]$$

Where W is the winning probability and R is the win/loss ratio.

The output of the equation is a number less than one or, in percentage form, what is called the Kelly percentage.

The percentage that the equation produces represents the size of the positions you should be taking. For example, if the Kelly percentage is 0.05, then you should take a trade with no more than 5% of your total trading capital per trade.

The system does require some common sense, however. One rule to keep in mind is that, regardless of what the Kelly percentage may tell you, commit no more than 20–25% of your capital to one trade. Allocating any more than this carries far more risks than most people should be taking.

The percentage figure spat out from the equation is often called a full Kelly. But many traders prefer to take trades with half of the Kelly percentage or even a quarter of the Kelly. For example, if the Kelly percentage turns out to be 5% (or 0.05 as in the example above), then a half Kelly would mean that you would be trading with 2.5% of your trading capital per trade. Similarly, for a quarter Kelly, you would be trading no more than 1.25% of your trading capital per trade.

As mentioned in Chapter 6, I have suggested that you trade with less than 1% of your trading capital per trade. But the Kelly system provides a different perspective of what percentage of your trading capital you should be using per trade. The idea is that you should be using only a percentage of your trading capital that you feel comfortable with.

Martingale System

Martingale is not strictly a money management system but a progressive trading methodology in which if the last trade is profitable after a string of losses, then you will recover all the lost investments in the previous trades plus the profit of the first trade. Trading binary options using the martingale strategy is a contentious subject with many traders as a continued string of losses can completely deplete a trading account. However, it is possible that, for certain trading opportunities and strategies, it can be an effective way to successfully use an increased probability of success to an advantage.

Please see the table below for one possible progression using the martingale system. The table assumes that the first trade to be 1% of your total trading capital and the return is 81% of your investment per trade, as offered by IG Markets. The minimum investment per trade of $37 as applicable for IG Markets has been assumed for the purpose of illustration.

Trade #	Investment per trade	Profit	Total return	Net profit, martingale	Cumulative investment	Return on investment	% of capital at risk
1	37	29.97	66.97	29.97	37	81.0%	1.0%
2	83	66.97	149.65	29.97	120	25.0%	3.2%
3	185	149.65	334.40	29.97	304	9.8%	8.2%
4	413	334.40	747.24	29.97	717	4.2%	19.4%
5	923	747.24	1,669.76	29.97	1,640	1.8%	44.3%
6	2,061	1,669.76	3,731.20	29.97	3,701	0.8%	100.0%
7	4,606	3,731.20	8,337.61	29.97	8,308	0.4%	224.5%
8	10,293	8,337.61	18,630.96	29.97	18,601	0.2%	502.7%
9	23,001	18,630.96	41,632.14	29.97	41,602	0.1%	1124.4%
10	51,398	41,632.14	93,029.85	29.97	93,000	0.0%	2513.5%

Table 3 Typical trade progression with martingale system

As obvious from the table above, essentially, martingale trading involves increasing the stake after each loss in order to increase the returns when the winning trade eventually comes in, with the understanding that a winning trade will have to happen at some point of time.

As attractive as the martingale strategy may look to you, increasing the investment on each high-probability trading set-up is arguable matter. Note that even if you have a good trading system, such as the one discussed in the book, you could expect between 60% to 80% successful trades. That sounds a lot based on the discussion so far, but if you encounter a string of, say, four losses, your fifth trade will need you to invest an amount which when added to the previous lost investments adds to over 44% of your trading capital. If that trade turns out to be winner, you will recoup all your previous investments, and you will also earn a profit of the very first trade. In which case, your return on investment drops to just 1.8%, compared to 81% return if your first trade was successful. You might argue that it's a good idea that you recoup the previous investments plus eke out a profit. But let's say that your fifth trade also turns out to be a loser and you are going to place a trade for the sixth trade. In your sixth trade, you are going to have to invest an amount which will take away 100% of your trading capital. At this stage, I hope and pray that your sixth trade turns out to be a winner as if you happen to lose this trade, then you are left with no trading capital at all! I am not sure, how many traders have the nerve to do this, perhaps not many. Even if you happen to have the nerve to take the sixth trade, where 100% of your investment capital is at risk, it is no way an optimal money management system. As mentioned previously and also in this chapter, your investment per trade should not be more than 1% of your trading capital.

So what's the way out when using martingale system? Should I use this at all? I leave that to your discretion based on the risks mentioned above. If you happen to decide to trade using martingale system, I would recommend you do the following:

1. Trade with less than 1% of your trading capital per trade, preferably 0.5%. This will mean that you can continue to place trades even with a string of losses exceeding 4 to 5.

2. As mentioned before, if you hit a string of three losses in a day, quit trading for the day as there must be something wrong either with your decision process or the market. If you do so, you will lose less than 5% of your investment capital in three trades with martingale, but you will still have more than 95% of your capital to start trading the next day.

I hear you ask, am I likely to encounter four or five losses in a row with your recommended trading strategy? No one can say with absolute certainty that you will or will not encounter a string of so many losses in a row. Although chances of so many losses in a row is extremely small, that may happen once in a while, and when that happens, you would like to protect your capital first so that you can come back to trading later. You will be able to do so only when you follow the two suggestions made above.

d'Alembert's Method

Thanks to the eighteenth-century mathematician Jean le Rond d'Alembert, we now have a progressive trading system in which even if you have 50% successful trades, you may still be able to make profit. The progressive trading system is not as aggressive as the martingale system described in the previous section as the trading progression is additive or subtractive to the original investment amount and not multiplicative as in the martingale system. Let me explain what I mean by that.

In this trading system, you start with a fixed number as your incremental amount by which each subsequent trade will be increased or decreased, depending upon the previous trade being a loser or winner respectively. That incremental amount is calculated as follows:

Incremental amount = initial investment / rate of return per trade

With $37 as your starting trade and 81% return as offered by IG Markets, your incremental amount is going to be $45. With that, the trade progression is as per the table in the following page. Basically, the hypothetical results of the progression is as follows:

1. Trade 1 (initial investment amount): You lose.
2. Trade 2 (initial investment increased by $45): You lose.
3. Trade 3 (initial investment increased by $90): You win.
4. Trade 4 (initial investment decreased by $45): You win.
5. Trade 5 (initial investment increased by $90): You lose.
6. Trade 6 (initial investment increased by $135): You win.

One of the best things about this progressive trading system is that your investment per trade does not increase exponentially as it does with martingale. As such, even after you have a few losing trades, you are still trading with relatively smaller amount. Please see the column on the percentage of capital at risk in the table in the next page. Secondly, as mentioned before, if you happen to take even number of trades and as long as only 50% of those trades were successful, you will end up having a positive return, and that would be higher than the return you would have if your first trade was successful.

Trade #	Investment	Profit	Cumulative investment	Win (1) Loss (0)	Profit	Return on investment	Percentage of capital at risk
1	37	29.97	37	0	-37.00	81.0%	1.00%
2	82	66.42	119	0	-82.00	55.8%	3.22%
3	127	102.87	246	1	102.87	41.8%	6.65%
4	82	66.42	143	0	-82.00	46.4%	3.87%
5	127	102.87	270	0	-127.00	38.1%	7.30%
6	172	139.32	442	1	139.32	31.5%	11.95%
7	127	102.87	303	0	-127.00	34.0%	8.18%
8	172	139.32	475	1	139.32	29.3%	12.83%
9	127	102.87	335	0	-127.00	30.7%	9.07%
10	172	139.32	507	0	-172.00	27.5%	13.72%
11	217	175.77	724	1	175.77	24.3%	19.58%
12	172	139.32	549	1	139.32	25.4%	14.83%
13	127	102.87	409	1	102.87	25.1%	11.06%
14	82	66.42	307	1	66.42	21.7%	8.28%
15	37	29.97	240	0	-37.00	12.5%	6.49%
16	82	66.42	322	1	66.42	20.6%	8.71%
17	37	29.97	256	0	-37.00	11.7%	6.91%
18	82	66.42	338	1	66.42	19.7%	9.13%
19	37	29.97	271	0	-37.00	11.0%	7.33%
20	82	66.42	353	1	66.42	18.8%	9.55%

Table 4 Typical trade progression with d'Alembert's method

Please study the table above carefully and check for yourself the sequence of success and failed trades you are getting, and as long as half of those trades are successful, you can restart the trading with only the initial investment to restart the cycle.

The above three systems have been given here for you to understand the alternatives available for managing your investment and trade with an amount in which you can minimize your risks. You could also use a combination of the two systems to optimize your risk/reward. For example, you may use half Kelly system with d'Alembert's method of progressive trading. In that way, you are keeping your initial investment low enough to implement a progressive trading to recover any potential losses.

Please review the above table, and make your own decision to implement a strategy of your choice based on your personal investment goals, risk appetite, and expectation of return.

— **End of Chapter 11** —

CHAPTER 12

My Trading Statements

As mentioned at the beginning of the book, the whole trading system described in the book was put to a test, and I have personally gone through all these at various stages of development of the trading method described to you. This is where the rubber meets the road, so they say.

Figures 47 below shows typical statements received from IG Markets daily, containing the previous day's trading results. It usually hits your inbox at about 8 a.m. AEST.

CLOSED POSITIONS AND LEDGER TRANSACTIONS IN AUSTRALIAN DOLLARS

Date	Deal Code	Details	Shares Buy (+) Sell (-)	Opening Level	Closing Level	Amt Due to you or us (-)
14MAR14		BROUGHT FORWARD				10,302.57
		CLOSING TRADES				
14MAR14	YYG3AP	USD/JPY to be above 10162.9 at 14:25:00 14/03/14 YRBFAN is now completely closed.	37	10162.9	10164.300000	29.97
14MAR14	YEDRAP	USD/JPY to be above 10177.1 at 12:05:00 14/03/14 YNWUA2 is now completely closed.	37	10177.1	10177.400000	29.97
14MAR14	YD7KAP	USD/JPY to be above 10175.9 at 11:10:00 14/03/14 X444AR is now completely closed.	37	10175.9	10178.100000	29.97
14MAR14	YEJ3AP	USD/JPY to be above 10177.7 at 12:45:01 14/03/14 YHZXAU is now completely closed.	37	10177.7	10181.500000	29.97
14MAR14	YYABAP	USD/JPY to be above 10181.6 at 13:25:00 14/03/14 YNARAH is now completely closed.	37	10181.6	10182.200000	29.97
16MAR14		CARRIED FORWARD				10,452.42

CLOSED POSITIONS AND LEDGER TRANSACTIONS IN AUSTRALIAN DOLLARS

Date	Deal Code	Details	Shares Buy (+) Sell (-)	Opening Level	Closing Level	Amt Due to you or us (-)
10FEB14		BROUGHT FORWARD				10,615.29
		CLOSING TRADES				
10FEB14	6RBCAJ	GBP/USD to be above 16409.8 at 10:40:00 10/02/14 6X25AW is now completely closed.	37	16409.8	16410.900000	29.97
10FEB14	7PWRAJ	GBP/USD to be above 16413.1 at 13:49:40 10/02/14 7GGJAK is now completely closed.	83	16413.1	16414.800000	67.23
10FEB14	6RF8AJ	GBP/USD to be above 16408.5 at 11:05:01 10/02/14 6SCVAY is now completely closed.	37	16408.5	16413.000000	29.97
10FEB14	7AA2AJ	GBP/USD to be above 16408.3 at 11:55:01 10/02/14 7AQ4AP is now completely closed.	37	16408.3	16409.200000	29.97
10FEB14	7AFVAJ	GBP/USD to be above 16411.1 at 12:20:01 10/02/14 67YDAS is now completely closed.	37	16411.1	16412.800000	29.97
10FEB14	7AH5AJ	GBP/USD to be above 16407.8 at 12:40:06 10/02/14 7LZVAN is now completely closed.	37	16407.8	16408.800000	29.97
10FEB14	7APFAJ	GBP/USD to be above 16411.5 at 13:30:01 10/02/14 7SYUAD is now completely closed.	37	16411.5	16411.800000	29.97
10FEB14		CARRIED FORWARD				10,862.34

Figure 47: IG Markets' daily statement sent via email.

The statement in the previous page shows consecutive successful trades on both days' statement. Don't worry, this is not typical. Most likely you will have a few days when you will have all successful trades. Some days you will have a mix of some successful and failed trades. And in some days, it may just be average. The key is to stick to the discipline and keep on trading so that on an average, you have more winning trades than losing ones by some margin. This way, you will see your account growing, or at least, you are making a steady daily income. Also note that I was trading two other currency pairs, viz. GBPUSD and USDJPY. As mentioned in Chapter 2, both these currency pairs are the second and third highest traded pairs and are quite volatile for trading using the strategy suggested in this book. I would recommend that beginners start trading EURUSD only after gaining confidence to try other pairs such as here.

As discussed in the previous chapter, martingale has been quite popular among some traders as it looks like a very attractive proposition. Most traders continue to use it till the time they get hit by a single bad trading day and a significant portion of their capital is wiped out because of the disproportionate amount of money being put in one trade. At some stage, a trader is forced to break the golden rule of trading just to recover only the profit that would have come from the first trade, had that been successful. I am reproducing below one of my own statements that shows how the progression went.

CLOSED POSITIONS AND LEDGER TRANSACTIONS IN AUSTRALIAN DOLLARS

Date	Deal Code	Details	Shares Buy (+) Sell (-)	Opening Level	Closing Level	Amt Due to you or us (-)
24FEB14		BROUGHT FORWARD				11,599.98
		CLOSING TRADES				
24FEB14	PHWKA8	EUR/USD to be above 13739.1 at 10:30:00 24/02/14 PNSGBD is now completely closed.	37	13739.1	13739.700000	29.97
24FEB14	Q9BVA8	EUR/USD to be above 13734.2 at 14:55:02 24/02/14 O4JXAQ is now completely closed.	37	13734.2	13735.900000	29.97
24FEB14	P6WHA8	EUR/USD to be above 13737.4 at 12:10:01 24/02/14 P8DRAP is now completely closed.	37	13737.4	13735.900000	-37.00
24FEB14	P6XCA8	EUR/USD to be above 13735.9 at 12:15:00 24/02/14 QEE2AZ is now completely closed.	83	13735.9	13735.900000	-41.50
24FEB14	OQ2FA8	EUR/USD to be above 13735.9 at 12:19:59 24/02/14 P9UDAX is now completely closed.	185	13735.9	13733.600000	-185.00
24FEB14	OQ2ZA8	EUR/USD to be above 13733.6 at 12:24:59 24/02/14 Q4JMGAH is now completely closed.	413	13733.6	13733.700000	334.53
24FEB14	OQ77A8	EUR/USD to be above 13731.4 at 12:55:02 24/02/14 QF4AAF is now completely closed.	37	13731.4	13729.600000	-37.00
24FEB14	OQ84A8	EUR/USD to be above 13729.8 at 13:00:04 24/02/14 QNTLBC is now completely closed.	83	13729.8	13730.600000	67.23
24FEB14		CARRIED FORWARD				11,761.18

Figure 48: My trading statement with the martingale system.

In Figure 48, note that I have lost three consecutive trades, but the fourth trade turned out to be a winner, recovering all that I had invested in three previous trades plus the original profit I was expecting from the first trade.

Please note that this statement was sent to me after I traded in a manner to show martingale trading progression at work. As mentioned before, a trader needs to take a break for the day after three consecutive losses, but in this case, I continued to trade to demonstrate the effect, and as it turned out, the fourth trade was a winner. If the fourth trade was unsuccessful and I had to place a trade for the fifth trade in the martingale progression, then I would be putting a trade for $923. That could be a significant percentage of your trading account, depending on how much money is in your trading account.

A far safer approach for trading is the d'Alembert's progression method. And this is one method where even if you have only 50% successful trade in a day, you will end up having a profit, contrary to what I had told you in Chapter 1! The only requirement here is that you will have to keep on taking trades till you reach a point where the number of winners is the same as the number of losers. Refer to Chapter 11 for the progression table.

I am reproducing my trading statement in the following page where you can see the effect of d'Alembert's progression. The statement in Figure 49 has actually a mix of martingale system and d'Alembert's progression. The third, fourth, and fifth transactions from the top show the martingale progression whereas lower few transactions is an incomplete progression of the d'Alembert's system.

CLOSED POSITIONS AND LEDGER TRANSACTIONS IN AUSTRALIAN DOLLARS

Date	Deal Code	Details	Shares Buy (+) Sell (-)	Opening Level	Closing Level	Amt Due to you or us (-)
20MAR14	YVANAP	USDJPY to be above 10225.4 at 16:15:00 20/03/14 YSXOAC is now completely closed.	37	10225.4	10228.200000	29.97
20MAR14	YVBXAP	USDJPY to be below 10231.9 at 16:30:00 20/03/14 YTG2AW is now completely closed.	37	10231.9	10230.800000	29.97
20MAR14	YVO9AP	USDJPY to be above 10228.1 at 16:44:59 20/03/14 YRL3A4 is now completely closed.	37	10228.1	10229.000000	29.97
20MAR14	ZU9QAP	USDJPY to be below 10236.3 at 19:05:00 20/03/14 ZUNGAH is now completely closed.	37	10236.8	10240.800000	-37.00
20MAR14	2DZSAP	USDJPY to be below 10240.8 at 19:09:59 20/03/14 Z9KTAW is now completely closed.	83	10240.8	10241.100000	-83.00
20MAR14	2D5LAP	USDJPY to be below 10240.9 at 19:14:59 20/03/14 Z26PAN is now completely closed.	185	10240.9	10237.800000	149.85
20MAR14	4C3OAP	USDJPY to be below 10241.8 at 20:40:00 20/03/14 3YSCAK is now completely closed.	37	10241.8	10241.900000	-37.00
20MAR14	YD5MAP	USDJPY to be below 10244.1 at 13:20:02 20/03/14 X8ENBD is now completely closed.	37	10244.1	10245.800000	-37.00
20MAR14	YD5YAP	USDJPY to be below 10245.6 at 13:25:00 20/03/14 YHGRB8 is now completely closed.	83	10245.6	10244.600000	67.23
20MAR14	YD66AP	USDJPY to be above 10242.4 at 13:40:00 20/03/14 X7LBA8 is now completely closed.	37	10242.4	10241.500000	-37.00
20MAR14	YD7FAP	USDJPY to be above 10241.4 at 13:45:01 20/03/14 YF22BC is now completely closed.	83	10241.4	10240.600000	-83.00
20MAR14		CARRIED FORWARD				11,030.57

Figure 49: My trading statement with d'Alembert's system.

So you now have a good idea of how a trading statement looks like after you have deployed the trading strategy described in this book. If you are with a different broker, your trading statement may look different, but you get the idea. You also have seen that I had actually implemented the money management scheme and progressive trading in my daily trading. These should give you an idea of what to expect when you start trading also the confidence on using the methodology described in the book.

— **End of Chapter 12** —

CHAPTER 13

A Four-Week Action Plan

Congratulations! You have made it to this chapter after having read the previous one. Here is where the rubber meets the road. But how? Most likely you are alone in your journey and not sure of how you go from here. Is there a fellow next to you to discuss anything that you have read and learnt from this book? If yes, then good for you. You can always bounce your ideas off that person, share the learning, and exchange views. If not, you are on your own, but don't despair; that's life. We do start most of our journey alone and finish alone, but on our way, we play our role and have plenty of memories with our family, friends, colleagues, and people around us. You may draw inspiration from me as well as I learnt all these alone, but I had Sumita to share my thoughts and my learning with. She was someone from whom I could seek views on my journey.

Now that you have learnt a new skill and perhaps are very keen to jump into action, I think you need to have an overall plan as to how you want to bring this whole skill into real life This is a big-picture plan, unlike the plan we discussed in Chapter 6. The purpose of this four-week action plan is to ensure that you are fully prepared and have gone through some of the basics before you are on your way.

In this chapter, I will lay out an action plan that you can use to get underway or at least give you a road map of suggested actions before you get into action.

Like every other activity that you want to embark upon, you will need to set aside certain hours of a working day for trading. If you live in Australia, the best trading hours of the day is from 9 a.m. till 4 p.m. Australian Eastern Standard Time (AEST) if you trade EURUSD as described in the book. I have created a table to make sure that you are aware of the times in your city so that you could set aside the appropriate hours. Please see Table 5 in the following page for your local time. If you live in another city not listed, please pick your nearest city and make suitable adjustments in trading hours with respect to your nearest city listed in the table.

If the times mentioned in Table 5 do not work for you, you might consider trading the other asset, USDJPY. For the type of trading discussed in this book, the best trading hours for USDJPY is from 5 p.m. to 11 p.m. AEST. I have also created another table for you for the equivalent times in your local cities. Please see Table 6.

Table 5 EURUSD Trading hours

Sydney	9 a.m. to 4 p.m.
Berlin	1 a.m. to 8 a.m.
Buenos Aires	8 p.m. to 3 a.m.
Dallas	6 p.m. to 1 a.m.
Johannesburg	1 a.m. to 8 a.m.
Kuwait City	2 a.m. to 9 a.m.
London	midnight to 7 a.m.
New Delhi	4.30 a.m. to 11.30 a.m.
New York	7 p.m. to 2 a.m.
San Francisco	4 p.m. to 9 p.m.
Tokyo	8 a.m. to 3 p.m.
Washington DC	7 p.m. to 2 a.m.

I hope one of these times work for you. If you are lucky and can afford to make a choice between the two trading hours, pick the one that least disrupts your normal life.

Table 6 USDJPY trading hours

Sydney	5 p.m. to midnight
Berlin	9 a.m. to 4 p.m.
Buenos Aires	4 a.m. to 11 a.m.
Dallas	2 a.m. to 9 a.m.
Johannesburg	9 a.m. to 4 p.m.
Kuwait City	10 a.m. to 5 p.m.
London	8 a.m. to 3 p.m.
New Delhi	12.30 p.m. to 7 p.m.
New York	3 a.m. to 10 a.m.
San Francisco	midnight to 7 a.m.
Tokyo	4 p.m. to 11 p.m.
Washington DC	3 a.m. to 10 a.m.

With the trading times out of the way, I would like to mention here that you are not expected to be trading on all these hours every day; otherwise, it becomes another job. So you will perhaps take a few trades for as long it takes to complete it, and then you are out of it for the day. And that may happen only in the first hour or a couple of hours so that you can spend time doing the things that you want to do and are passionate about.

Most experienced traders suggest that if you have three winning trades in a row, you should be out of trading for the day as you have a life to live and enjoy. Similarly, if you have three losses in a row, you will need to stop trading for the day. Three losses in a row mean that your decision-making process on that day has not been very sound or the market is being very choppy and not respecting the support and resistances. In case of losses, you should not be in the market any longer than that as the trading environment is not conducive, and you need to take a break before you go back to trading.

The break helps you get over the emotion of loss, and it gives you time to analyze the reason for your losses and revisit the rules of trading if required. The break will help you resurrect your trading skill and will let you come back to trading with a fresh mind rather than one still thinking about the losses you made. As mentioned many times throughout the book, it is about putting the odds in your favour, and hence, winning and losing will continue to travel with you all along your journey. All you need to do is keep calm and continue trading in such a manner that the number of winners over a period of time is more than the number of losers so that you can make a net profit.

The following is a blueprint of the action plan from day 1 after you finished reading the book, spanning over the four weeks:

Week 1: Ascertain what type of person you are and whether or not you have the temperament to invest time and effort to do something like this. In other words, what's your level of drive to venture into trading in financial markets and desire to be successful? If you are determined to be successful and willing to do whatever it takes, then invest a few minutes in a day to do some breathing exercises. Start from day 1 and continue to do that for the next five days. Breathing exercises helps you calm down your mind, learn to focus on one thing at a time, and remove your mind from distractions. This is a key to trading as you will be required to make decisions in a relatively short time after analyzing a variety of situations. The breathing exercise is best done certain times of the day, but you will need to be doing this exercise every day before you start trading. You may choose to do that two times a day as well—in the morning and in the evening.

Week 2: Once you have learnt the breathing exercises and settled in doing it continuously for five days, revisit the chapters one at a time per day, starting from Chapter 6. Revisit all the tools mentioned therein, get to the bottom of each, and get very clear about each of the tools, one tool in a day.

Look at the charts in the book, and get a mental picture of how the asset price in the market moved over time or every five minutes. Remember, the charts are just a visual of billions of dollars of buying and selling taking place in the market, and you are going to be one of the participants in that market however small or large the amount of your investment is going to be. So getting to know the charts are as important as knowing the streets in your neighbourhood to get home in your suburb.

As mentioned in the chapter on candlesticks, reading the market psychology through candlestick is a great skill to learn. Please devote at least one full day studying the shapes of the candles, their sizes, and the way the market price moved following the formation of a certain candle. If you are able to learn to predict the price movement following the close of the previous candle, you have reached a significant milestone in your trading career. If you need to practise the candlestick in a real-life environment, that will follow soon, but get yourself familiar with the other tools that were mentioned in Chapter 6 as well.

Week 3: This is a critical week for you as you will now start to put into practice your learning over the last two weeks and the understanding you had from reading the book. You will do this with paper money or fake money to put a trade and see the result. Some of the brokers of binary options offer a practice account with a certain amount of fake money for practice before you put real money into the account and start trading. Practice account is optional, and you will need to ask for it while you open an account.

IG Markets offers a trial account for two weeks only with $50,000 fake money in the account. You do not need to put any real money into the account. Just open the account with your name, address, and other credentials, and you are ready to practise trading with paper money. Please note that IG Markets is the only broker which has a trading platform with a built-in charting facility. That's one of the reasons I personally prefer IG Markets as the broker provides a full-featured trading facility. If your broker does not provide a trial account with paper money, you still can practise placing trades, except that you place the trade in your mind and make a note to that effect in a trading journal or a notebook.

Whichever way you decide to go, once you signed up with a broker of your choice and the account is set up with practice money, please proceed with setting up the chart and trading platform as mentioned in Chapter 8. As mentioned in Chapter 6, Tool No. 1, please make sure that the timer you are using is synced with the trading platform clock and that the alert goes off around 30 to 40 seconds before the clock hits every 5-minute mark.

With this preparation, you are ready to place your first trade on the practice account with paper money. Wait for the alert to go off. When it does, you have around 30 to 40 seconds to make a decision to place the trade. If you are satisfied that a set-up exists and you anticipate the price movement, *up* or *down*, in the next 20 minutes, please proceed to place a trade as discussed in Chapter 9 with an investment of $100 per trade. Place as many trades as possible based on your assessment of the chart and whether or not a set-up exists.

Please continue trading with paper money for at least one week or five working days. Please document each trade of these five days in a journal—the time of day, the trade direction, and the reason you took the trade. At the end of the week or after the five working days, which should be a Saturday (assuming your starting day of week 3 is Monday), analyze the trades by looking back at the chart and check if the winning and losing trades were actually placed as per the set-up. Make notes on your journal about those trades so that you can revisit that in the future if needed.

Week 4: This is the last week of our four-week action plan. You might want to maximize your learning so far and gain confidence on placing trades following the set-ups discussed in this book as the practice account is available only until this week if you are with IG Markets. With the learning from last week and after revisiting last week's trade, you are better prepared to take more trades this week. Continue to look for set-ups that are near perfect, and take those trades. Check your success rate at the end of each day, and continue to document each and every trade as you would have done last week so that you can go through them to understand if any mistakes were made. It is likely that you had made some mistakes or the market behaved in a manner that caught you off guard. You will need to learn from those mistakes and make notes on what and how they happened and the measures you will take to prevent that from happening again.

This is the week when you might want to test some of the money management systems discussed in Chapter 11. You will need to prepare a table similar to the ones in Chapter 11 for the amount of your initial investment, and then use the progressive trading system that you would like to try. This will also give you an idea of how these systems work, and if you would like to use it in your real-money trading, you would know what to expect.

By the end of week 4, you would have developed a fair amount of confidence on how you can use all the tools at your disposal to place a trade and increase your capital. If you think that you need a few more days or weeks to gain more confidence before you place a trade with real money, you may ask your broker to extend the trial account for two more weeks. If they agree to do that, then you are fine to practise for additional weeks, but if not, then please place trades mentally while documenting the trade in a journal as you would have done in the last two weeks. But I sincerely hope that you would be well prepared within the four weeks to start trading with real money.

Please do not despair if you haven't had enough practice for the whole duration of two weeks. Life has not always prepared us to face everything that we have come across in our life, but we have learnt to handle those and have come a long way. You might have a few hiccups here and there, and that's perfectly normal as long as you know what you are doing.

— End of Chapter 13 —

FURTHER READING

Baiynd, Anne-Marie, *The Trading Book: A Complete Solution to Mastering Technical Analysis and Trading Psychology.*

Nison, Steve, *Japanese Candlestick Charting Techniques.*

Thomsett, Michael C., *Support & Resistance Simplified (Simplified Series Book 7)*

Elder, Alexander *Trading for a Living: Psychology, Trading Tactics, Money Management*

INDEX